I0411562

TABLE OF CONTENTS

i

ACRONYMS

ADM   Army Design Methodology

BH   Boko Haram

CAF   Conflict Assessment Framework

GAI   Guide for the Analysis of Insurgency

ICAF   Interagency Conflict Assessment Framework

MEND   Movement for the Emancipation of the Niger Delta

MNLA   National Movement for the Liberation of Azawad

MOSOP   Movement for the Survival of the Ogoni People

NDPVF   Niger Delta People's Volunteer Force

USAID   United States Agency for International Development

ILLUSTRATIONS

TABLES

It is true that America cannot use our military wherever repression occurs. And given the costs and risks of intervention, we must always measure our interests against the need for action.

—President Barack Obama

INTRODUCTION

This monograph seeks to determine how military planners should perform assessments of insurgencies during phase zero - before the commitment to major military operations. Throughout this study, major military operations will mean operations intended to effect a change in the insurgency or its environment. Three assessment frameworks - the Interagency Conflict Assessment Framework, the Guide for the Analysis of Insurgency, and the Army Design Methodology - are tested against three case studies - Boko Haram of Nigeria, the Movement for the Emancipation of the Niger Delta of Nigeria, and the National Movement for the Liberation of Azawad of Mali. The initial study hypothesis holds that the Interagency Conflict Assessment Framework, owing to its whole-of-government inclusiveness, will prove most helpful to decision makers in creating or modifying United States policy to affected areas.

Context of the Study

The Council on Foreign Relations fixes the number of ongoing insurgencies at seventy.[1] Some begin and end without much interest from the United States. Others captivate the international community as with Afghanistan and Syria. The specific explanations for why and how insurgencies proliferate are not always clear. What is clear is that insurgency is not anomalous and represents a consistent challenge to United States national security objectives.

The United States government plays a role, large or small, in every insurgency. Simply put, it either acts on the situation or chooses inaction. This statement does not imply that there is an articulation of a national interest in every insurgency, it merely acknowledges the United

---

[1]Max Boot, Invisible Armies Insurgency Tracker (Council on Foreign Relations, 2013), http://www.cfr.org/wars-and-warfare/invisible-armies-insurgency-tracker/p29917 (accessed September 25, 2013).

States' demonstrated willingness to act in select cases around the world. This willingness to act then brings every case into question. Strategic dialogue within the national security apparatus reinforces the importance of responding to insurgency in its many forms. The military includes countering terrorism, irregular warfare, and insurgency among its primary missions.[2] The United States remains the preeminent coercive force and lead security provider in the world. Regardless of the precise manner that the United States chooses to weigh in, it always plays a role in the legitimization or de-legitimization of movements; even ignorance or inaction makes a statement.

Resources limit the United States' freedom of action with respect to insurgency. The United States spends more on its military than the next thirteen highest spenders combined.[3] In spite of this massive investment, even the world's lone superpower must choose its commitments carefully. It simply does not possess the resources to operate in all places where interests present themselves. In particular, policymakers are keenly aware of the cost of large-scale involvement in insurgency operations. Iraq and Afghanistan demonstrated the United States' ability to operate in support of and in opposition to insurgent forces. They also demonstrated the immense draw on personnel and finances brought on by such campaigns. These resource constraints exist regardless of national economic fortunes, but they become more acute during economic downturns and weaker tax revenues. The enactment of the Budget Control Act of 2011 brought this tension into sharper focus. Typically positive and understated, even the current Defense Strategic Guidance document calls attention to these challenges and seeks ways to maintain capability while reducing the "cost of doing business."[4] The need for judicious use of military and interagency community resources becomes ever clearer with these reductions.

---

[2]U.S. Department of Defense, *Sustaining U.S. Global Leadership: Priorities for 21st Century Defense* (Washington, DC: Government Printing Office, 2012), 4.

[3]Brad Plumer, "America's Staggering Defense Budget in Charts," *Washington Post*, January 7, 2013, http://www.washingtonpost.com/blogs/wonkblog/wp/2013/01/07/everything-chuck-hagel-needs-to-know-about-the-defense-budget-in-charts/ (accessed September 5, 2013).

[4]U.S. Department of Defense, 7.

This study argues that the military must provide useful assessments of insurgencies before the commitment to military operations - during phase zero. Policymakers recognize the impossibility of prescience in all areas of conflict. They further recognize that other members of the interagency community bear the responsibility to provide assessments. These caveats notwithstanding, the military plays an important role. It represents the capacity to act kinetically in support of the insurgency or in support of the incumbent. It must therefore be the lead agent for the risks and opportunities for the military instrument in any given scenario. The military must not only elaborate the use of its own instrument, but it must clearly understand the environment and the other instruments that may be brought to bear on the situation.

Study Design

The study consists of four parts. It begins with a literature review that describes the assessment frameworks to be evaluated. It then outlines the study methodology. Next, it applies the frameworks to the case studies and evaluates the effectiveness of each approach. It concludes with recommendations.

This study meets with success if it compares insurgency assessments successfully. A working knowledge of which assessments provide valuable input to policymakers gives military planners a place to begin in their efforts to support decisions. Getting the right knowledge to policymakers at the right time and in the right format ranks among the foremost duties of the military planner.

> Do we really know so little about the causes of riot and rebellion that we must invoke contemporary exorcisms like "aggressive instincts" or "conspiracy" to explain them? I think not.
>
> —Ted Robert Gurr

LITERATURE REVIEW

This study reviews knowledge in service of three ends: to better understand the assessment methodologies under review, to better understand the way leaders make decisions about insurgency and intervention, and to better understand the phenomenon of insurgency. Part one of this chapter reviews knowledge of the methodologies themselves. The information captured in this part puts the methodologies in perspective. It also informs their application in the analysis chapter yet to come. Part two reviews sources of information used in decision making. This section does not attempt to evaluate decision theory or exhaustively study particular decisions about insurgency. The goal is to support evaluation. Observing the inputs used in decisions about insurgency allows a more informed evaluation of the utility of each framework to decision makers. Part three reviews knowledge of the phenomenon of insurgency. For an insurgency assessment to be useful, it must facilitate the understanding of the phenomenon. This section aims to reveal the degree to which each methodology explains the phenomenon of insurgency. Overall, this chapter will provide a foundation for analysis and eventual evaluation.

A narrow band of scholarship surrounds the assessments reviewed in this study. The literature concerning each will be reviewed in turn. The three tools to be reviewed are the Interagency Conflict Assessment Framework, the Guide for the Analysis of Insurgency, and the Army Design Methodology. This chapter synthesizes the available information to build context and demonstrate the strengths and weaknesses that each methodology exhibits.

Interagency Conflict Assessment Framework

History

The Department of State developed the Interagency Conflict Assessment Framework, or ICAF, to address the problem of how the United States might contribute to peace and security in

4

war torn areas. This methodology therefore correlates strongly with the goal of this study.

Members of the interagency community use it frequently, and the authors of the framework

specifically designed it for a whole-of-government approach and for a wide variety of potential

uses: Department of Defense security cooperation planning, country team assessments to

missions, and conflict management.[5] This methodology's important role invites consideration

here.

National Security Presidential Directive Forty-Four acted as the catalyst for development.

That document mandated that planners focus on "at risk" areas, thus requiring greater assessment

and prevention efforts.[6] The ICAF evolved from its predecessor, the United States Agency for

International Development's (USAID) Conflict Assessment Framework (CAF) in 2007.[7] While

both methodologies apply to areas of conflict, the ICAF specifically seeks to corral the inputs of

various members of the interagency community into usable assessments of ongoing conflicts. In

its own words

> The Interagency Conflict Assessment Framework (ICAF) is a tool that enables a
> team comprised of a variety of USG agency representatives ("interagency") to assess
> conflict situations systematically and collaboratively and prepare for interagency
> planning for conflict prevention, mitigation, and stabilization.[8]

After the joint State Department and USAID team authored the methodology, an

interagency community working group then tested it for the first time in 2008 with an evaluation

of Tajikistan. It has been used many times since.

---

[5]Dane Smith, *Foreign Assistance for Peace: The U.S. Agency for International Development* (Washington, DC: Center for Strategic and International Studies, 2009), http://www.voltairenet.org/IMG/pdf/USAID.pdf 17 (accessed January 10, 2014).

[6]Hans Binnendijk and Patrick M. Cronin, eds., *Civilian Surge: Key to Complex Operations* (Washington, DC: Published for the Center for Technology and National Security Policy by National Defense University Press, 2009), 99.

[7]Smith, 17.

[8]U.S. Department of State, Office of the Coordinator for Reconstruction and Stabilization, *The Interagency Conflict Assessment Framework* (Washington, DC: S/CRS, 2008), 1.

Overview

The ICAF follows a simple process consisting of two tasks. The first task, called Conflict Diagnosis, consists of four steps:

Step One: Evaluate the Context of the Conflict

Step Two: Understand Core Grievances and Social/Institutional Resilience

Step Three: Identify Drivers of Conflict and Mitigating Factors

Step Four: Describe Opportunities for Increasing or Decreasing Conflict

The second task is to segue into planning. This task can provide input into three types of follow-on planning: steady state engagement/conflict prevention planning, reconstruction and stabilization contingency planning, or crisis response planning. The differences between these types of planning lie in the current status of the conflict, United States government participation in the conflict, and the time horizon available for planning.[9] In each case, the general goal is the same: to develop a shared understanding of a given conflict and provide a foundation for further planning.

Commentary

Observers point to the inclusive nature of the ICAF as an example of its utility as a whole-of-government approach to problem solving. Much like the Army Design Methodology, the ICAF contains relatively few steps. The spare nature leaves room for the user to innovate and use a wide variety of tools as subroutines. The "systems map" process recommended by ICAF practitioners exemplifies the usage of these subroutines.[10]

---

[9]United States Department of State, *The Interagency Conflict Assessment Framework,* 4.

[10]U.S. Department of State, "Philippines: Looking at Mindanao," *ICAF Report*, January 2011, 5, http://www.state.gov/documents/organization/187972.pdf (accessed 4 May 2012).

"Mapping the system" strongly resembles what Jamshid Gharajedaghi calls "mapping the mess."[11] According to Gharajedaghi, this activity enables the systems analyst to make sense of obstructions and interactions within the system under scrutiny. The ICAF does not direct that practitioners *must* employ this subroutine, but best practices indicate that it provides useful understanding. According to Dr. Cynthia Irmer, one of the ICAF's original authors, this focus on systems thinking and complex, adaptive systems differentiates the framework from pre-existing linear tools and makes it useful for studying insurgency.[12] Writing for the U.S. Army's Command and General Staff College, Majors James Wilson and Anthony Poole concur that the ICAF applies well to complex systems. Poole concludes that it meshes well with the Army Design Methodology and reinforces quality conceptual planning.[13] Wilson acknowledges the utility but caveats that quality intellectual habits are needed to complete the relatively open form ICAF.[14]

Conclusion

Overall, the ICAF shows promise in its integrative capacity and should remain relevant in this field for some time to come. The applicability to complex, adaptive systems makes the framework well suited to the study of insurgency. Moreover, the ICAF's authors developed it with the exact sorts of problems that insurgencies present. They engineered it to suit a variety of needs across the interagency community from the outset. Practitioners must take caution regarding the broad, unspecific format of the ICAF. Though this characteristic brings freedom to

---

[11]Jamshid Gharajedaghi, *Systems Thinking: Managing Chaos and Complexity*, 2nd ed. (Amsterdam, NL: Elsevier, 2006), 135.

[12]Cynthia Irmer, "A Systems Approach and the Interagency Conflict Assessment Framework (ICAF)," in *The Cornwallis Group XIV Workshop: Analysis of Societal Conflict and Counter-Insurgency* (Vienna, Austria: The Cornwallis Group, 2009), 170, http://www.thecornwallisgroup.org /workshop_2009.php (accessed 22 September, 2013).

[13]Anthony Poole, "The Interagency Conflict Assessment Framework: A Pragmatic Tool for Army Design" (monograph, School of Advanced Military Studies, 2010), 45.

[14]James Wilson "Improving the Interagency Conflict Assessment Framework (ICAF) with Intellectual Habits" (master's thesis, Command and General Staff College, 2012), 66.

the practitioner to innovate, it also demands a significant level of skill. This skill is necessary to ensure that the assessment takes all relevant variables into account.

Guide for the Analysis of Insurgency

History

The origins of the Guide for the Analysis of Insurgency (GAI), are somewhat obscured by secrecy. The Central Intelligence Agency authored the approach sometime during the mid 1980s. Exact dates remain conspicuously absent. The guide remained classified until 2009. Following the declassification, it underwent a rewrite. The agency published the guide again in 2012 with a minimum of front matter to provide context. This monograph utilizes the 2012 version of the assessment in the comparison of methodologies.

Overview

The guide proposes a general method to study insurgencies. There are five sections to the guide: definitions, common characteristics of insurgency, common insurgent typologies, the life cycle of an insurgency and keys to analysis, and enduring qualities of insurgency and counterinsurgency. The guide establishes its intent to assist analysts in the analysis of insurgent conflict. In a statement that sounds simultaneous notes of caution and optimism, it lays out its own purpose:

> No two insurgencies are identical, and this Guide is not intended to provide a one-size-fits-all template. No insurgency is unique in all aspects, however, and most share some combination of characteristics, tactics, and objectives. Most pass through similar stages of development during their life cycle. These commonalities are the focus of this Guide, but analysts should note that the specific insurgencies they are examining will probably not exhibit all of the characteristics or undertake all of the activities addressed in the Guide.[15]

---

[15]U.S. Central Intelligence Agency, *Guide to the Analysis of Insurgency* (Washington, DC: Central Intelligence Agency, 2012), preface, https://www.hsdl.org/?view&did=713599 (accessed November 21, 2013).

Other methodologies present similar purpose statements, but the GAI demonstrates the most laser-like focus on the phenomenon of insurgency. This focus is congruent with the overall scheme of the document. It is an inside-out methodology: most of the lines of inquiry begin with the insurgent organization and work outwards to the context. The layout of the guide provides strong evidence to this point and mirrors the life cycle of an insurgency.[16]

Commentary

A lack of scholarship on the methodology prevents a complete review, but some analysis can be inferred. The evolution of the document from its 1980s predecessor provides useful commentary on perceived strengths and weaknesses over time. Continuities within the document reflect probable areas of institutional satisfaction with the tool. Significant continuities include overview materials, the overall structure of the methodology, sections on incipient and late stage insurgency, a section on counterinsurgency, and the net assessment. Changes represent probable areas of needed improvement, also as diagnosed by the institution. Significant changes include the addition of a section on pre-insurgency conditions, a section on resolution, and more summary materials. The section on determinants of control from the 1980s document found its way into the resolution section. Perhaps most significantly, the 2012 GAI is nearly twice the length of the original version. Therefore, the updates reflect not only a reordering, but a substantial augmentation to the contents. A chart reflecting the composition of the assessment follows.

---

[16]U.S. Central Intelligence Agency, table of contents.

Table 1: Content Comparison of GAI "1980s" and GAI 2012

	GAI "1980s"	GAI 2012
Front Matter	Scope Note Table of Contents	Preface Table of Contents
Overview	Insurgency Definition Common Insurgent Objectives Stages of an Insurgency Four Broad Categories	Definitions Common Characteristics Common Insurgent Typologies
Pre-insurgency		Life Cycle: Pre-insurgency Pre-existing Conditions Grievance Group Identity Recruitment and Training Arms and Supplies Government Reaction
Incipient Insurgency	Incipient Insurgency Organization and Recruitment Training Acquiring Resources Outside Support Popular Support Actions/Use of Violence	Life Cycle: Incipient Conflict Insurgent Leadership Theory of Victory Insurgent Unity Popular Support Insurgent Logistics Government Leadership Security Force Effectiveness External Support to Government
Determinants of Control	Determinants of Control in Insurgency Attitudes Organization Security	
Late Stage Insurgency	Late Stage: Successful Insurgency Progressive Loss of Support: Domestic Progressive Loss of Support: International Progressive Loss of Control Progressive Loss of Coercive Power	Life Cycle: Open Insurgency Political Factors Military Factors External Assistance
Counterinsurgency Approach	Effective Counterinsurgency Military Factors Non Military Factors	Counterinsurgency Approaches Population Centric Enemy Centric Authoritarian
Resolution		Resolution Stage Stalemate Insurgent Victory Negotiated Settlement Government Victory
Summary		Insurgency Life Cycle Chart Enduring Qualities of Insugency Counterinsurgency
Assessment	Net Assessment	Net Assessment
Miscellany		Appendix: Defining Insurgency

Source: Created by author from: U.S. Central Intelligence Agency, *Guide to the Analysis of Insurgency* (Washington, DC: Central Intelligence Agency, 2012), table of contents, https://www.hsdl.org/?view&did=713599 (accessed November 21, 2013); U.S. Central Intelligence Agency, *Guide to the Analysis of Insurgency* (Washington, DC: Central Intelligence Agency, date unknown), table of contents, https://www.hsdl.org/?view&did=230206 (accessed November 21, 2013).

Conclusion

Charles Locke, an instructor for the Central Intelligence Agency's Sherman Kent intelligence academy, teaches the methodology to the agency's analysts. He finds value in the process, but provides two cautions to ensure maximum value.[17] First, he suggests that the assessor begin at the level where insurgents are succeeding. Second, he warns that any student of insurgency should use more than one method to study this complex phenomenon. Significantly for this study, the Guide for the Analysis of Insurgency focuses mainly on the conduct of net assessments of insurgencies. This study seeks the most effective way for the military to do exactly that in advance of major operational commitments. It is also noteworthy that the GAI is the most detailed framework. The large amount of structure provides guidance to the user, but also constraint. This method begs for large amounts of data and takes fewer risks in the framing of the operational context.

Army Design Methodology

History

The Army Design Methodology evolved from its antecedent, Systemic Operational Design. The latter came into being during the mid 1990s in Israel. Brigadier General (Retired) Shimon Naveh developed the approach in an effort to address the complex phenomenon of warfare with the tools of systems theory.[18] The concept underwent significant intellectual ferment as the Israeli Defense Forces worked to institutionalize the principles. The United States Army took note of Systemic Operational Design in 2005, and sought General Naveh's assistance in exploring the concept. A group of officers from the School of Advanced Military Studies evaluated the approach, confirming its usefulness for planning. In 2007, the school incorporated

---

[17]Charles Locke, telephone interview with MAJ Michael Fogarty, Fort Leavenworth, KS, February 11, 2014.

[18]LTC William Sorrells et al., *Systemic Operational Design: An Introduction* (Fort Leavenworth, KS: United States Army Command and General Staff College, May 26, 2005), 8, www.dtic.mil/cgi-bin/GetTRDoc?AD=ADA479311 (accessed January 7, 2014).

Systemic Operational Design, or simply Design, into its core curriculum.[19] Since migrating from

the Israeli Defense Force to the United States Army, Systemic Operational Design underwent a

series of evolutions. An interim manual, Field Manual Interim 5-2: Design, first brought Design

into United States military doctrine.[20] With the rewritten Field Manual 5-0: the Operations

Process of March 2010, the Army formalized Design's place. The ferment continued. A successor

to Field Manual 5-0 was produced in 2011. The following year a broader reorganization of

doctrinal manuals led to the most comprehensive treatment of Design in companion publications

Army Doctrinal Manual 5-0 and Army Doctrinal Resource Publication 5-0. The pair replaced

Field Manual 5-0. Additionally, a series of guides and references were produced to improve

dissemination of Design within the force.[21] The consistent dialogue on Design resulted in a

methodology that departed from the original. The current version of Army Design Methodology

leverages military theory and history more significantly than earlier incarnations, and purports to

be less esoteric.

Overview

Design augments, rather than replaces, detailed planning methodologies like the Military

Decision Making Process within the Army system. Planners bring Design to bear to help solve

complex and ill-structured problems. Design focuses on appreciating problems in their holistic

being. Thus, it focuses predominantly on synthesis, where processes like the Military Decision

---

[19]U.S. Army, *Art of Design: Student Text, Version 2.0* (Fort Leavenworth, KS: United States Army Command and General Staff College, 2010), 3, http://usacac.army.mil/cac2/cgsc/ events/sams/artofdesign_v2.pdf (accessed February 17, 2014).

[20]COL Thomas Graves and Bruce Stanley, "Design and Operational Art: A Practical Approach to Teaching the Army Design Methodology", *Military Review* 93, no. 4 (July-August 2013), 54, http://usacac.army.mil/CAC2/MilitaryReview/Archives/English/MilitaryReview_20130831_art001.pdf (accessed December 10, 2013).

[21]Ibid, 55.

Making Process lean heavily on analysis for insights. The Army's Training and Doctrine Command Pamphlet 525-5-500 explains this dynamic well:

> Reductionism and analysis are not as useful with interactively complex systems because they lose sight of the dynamics between the components. The study of interactively complex systems must be *systemic* rather than reductionist, and qualitative rather than quantitative, and must use different heuristic approaches rather than analytical problem solving.[22]

This focus on the complex and holistic makes Design a suitable approach for considering insurgency.

The Army Design Methodology consists of three steps: environmental framing, problem framing, and developing an operational approach. Environmental framing is the first step, and sets the stage for the remainder of the process. This step seeks not to break down the environment into small pieces for analysis, but to scope the problem to a manageable scale and to appreciate the interactions and relationships within the environment.[23]

The second step, problem framing, establishes the nature of the problem to be solved. The problem frame captures the motivations and tensions of the parties identified within the system by the environmental frame.

The third step, developing an operational approach, seeks to provide the conceptual framework of a solution to the problem agreed upon in the previous step. This framework will provide direction and guidance for detailed planning activities. These activities can run concurrently with the Design process or follow sequentially.

---

[22]U.S. Army, Training and Doctrine Command Pamphlet 525-5-500, *Commander's Appreciation and Campaign Design*, 6.

[23]BG(P) Edward Cardon and LTC Steve Leonard, "Unleashing Design: Planning and the Art of Battle Command", *Military Review* 90, no. 2 (March-April 2010), 8, http://usacac.army.mil/CAC2/ MilitaryReview/Archives/English/MilitaryReview_20100430_art004.pdf (accessed February 17, 2014).

Commentary

Even its advocates admit that Design received a mixed reception throughout its

inculcation into military doctrine. The debate about Design's place centers on similar themes. Is

the methodology sound? Does it produce results that are useful in an operational setting? Does it

add value to existing planning systems or does it simply replicate many of the same functions?

Design enjoys many proponents, but has also faced harsh criticism from some. This section lays

out both cases with the aim of synthesizing key points in the literature to ascertain the value of the

methodology to this study.

Criticism of Design comes in two general varieties: outright rejection and skepticism. Its

harshest critics argue that Design is esoteric and based upon flawed principles. In his article "A

Case Against Systemic Operational Design" Milan Vego advises that the United States Military

not take up the banner of Systemic Operational Design from the Israelis. He argues that the

methodology was fundamentally unsound from the outset. It misconstrued its supposed

antecedents: Soviet operational art, French post-modern philosophy, and ancient Chinese military

texts.[24] Further, he argued that the process as developed by the Israelis ignored basic tenets of

operational planning, such as a defined end state, centers of gravity, and lines of operation. This

ignorance misled planners dangerously.[25] Gentler critiques of Design accept the theoretical

grounding but question its accessibility and its place within the broader operational planning

architecture. Writing for Tom Ricks' ForeignPolicy.com blog, Richard Buchanan admits that

Design may be an important part of the future, but regrets the messaging problems and the

difficulties encountered introducing the concept to the force.[26]

---

[24]Milan Vego, "A Case Against Systemic Operational Design," *Joint Forces Quarterly* 53, no. 2 (2nd quarter 2009), 70, www.dtic.mil/cgi-bin/GetTRDoc?AD=ADA515328: (accessed January 20, 2014).

[25]Ibid, 74.

[26]Richard Buchanan "Best Defense: Is the Army Design Methodology Over Designed?," *Foreign Policy*, November 1, 2012, http://ricks.foreignpolicy.com/posts/2012/11/01/is_army_design_methodology_over_designed_there_are_trust_issues_too (accessed February 7, 2014).

Conclusion

The Army Design Methodology is qualitatively different from, is inherently connected to, and provides added value to existing methodologies.[27] This is particularly true when considering complex and unfamiliar situations. These characteristics make this approach valuable to the study of an insurgency.

Decision Input

Who is a policymaker and what must they know to make sound decisions about acting upon an insurgency? A quality insurgency assessment should aim to answer those information requirements. The first half of the question requires relatively little elaboration. This study defines the term policymaker inclusively. Persons that act upon the nation's decisions to intervene in situations where insurgencies take place rate as policymakers. This definition applies mainly, but not exclusively, to elected or appointed senior officials of the United States government concerned with foreign policy. White House senior staff, key Congressional leaders, departmental secretaries and deputies warrant special attention given their central role in committing to intervention.

The question of what policymakers must know in the decision process becomes much more contentious. Intuition and national mood no doubt play a key role, but to define this role would require an entirely separate study. This study defines the information policymakers need to know as critical input to the decision process, or simply critical input. It derives from two sources: formal and informal. Public law, treaties, and policy documents provide a window into formal critical inputs that guide policymakers. Speeches, statements, and credible reports describe some of the informal critical inputs that guide decisions.

---

[27]Cardon and Leonard, 6.

Formal critical inputs tend to provide the advantage of clarity and legitimacy. Public law generally obliges policymakers to behave in a certain way, excepting cases of conflicting statute. A Congressional declaration of war exemplifies a statute requiring intervention, but the inquiry then must turn to the process that informed the declaration. Treaty obligations generally consist of specific triggers and activities that provide inherent decision criteria. The North Atlantic Treaty Organization Charter offers a clear manifestation. Article five of the charter stipulates that an attack on one of the member nations constitutes an attack on all members and activates the alliance.[28] The North Atlantic Council invoked the article only once - for the attacks of September 11th - but it resulted in immediate support from the member nations. That support continues twelve years later. Policies present somewhat murkier decision support. Policy can also offer guidelines for decision. President Ronald Reagan offered support to anti-communist rebels with the so-called "Reagan Doctrine" of 1985.[29] As with other policies, the doctrine remained open to interpretation concerning specifics of support, and disagreement persisted over implementation. The situation still required analysis. Perhaps most relevant to current and future decisions, United States government strategy documents indicate the landscape of national interests with the greatest fidelity. First among these, the National Security Strategy sets the tone for the others. The most recent version, published in 2010, lays out four enduring interests: security, prosperity, values, and international order.[30] A number of subordinate interests feed into each of these. The

---

[28]"NATO and the Scourge of Terrorism," NATO.int, February 18, 2005, http://www.nato.int/terrorism/five.htm (accessed February 5, 2014).

[29]Ted Galen Carpenter, *U.S. Aid to Anti-Communist Rebels: The "Reagan Doctrine" and Its Pitfalls* (Washington, DC: CATO Institute, 1986), http://www.cato.org/pubs/pas/pa074es.html, (accessed November 20, 2013).

[30]Barack Obama, *National Security Strategy: May 2010* (Washington, DC: United States government, 2010), 17, http://www.whitehouse.gov/sites/default/files/rss_viewer/national_security_strategy.pdf (accessed November 21, 2013).

essential value of all of these formal decision inputs lays in their power to illuminate the national interest, the heart of every decision about intervention in conflict.

Informal critical inputs - speeches and statements - provide a clearer window into the decision processes of key leaders. Presidential statements make for excellent examples. Former Reagan administration speechwriter John Roberts notes that a a significant process of vetting and feedback goes into every speech[31]. President Barack Obama gave clear reflections of his decision process in the Syrian insurgency:

> This is what's at stake. And that is why, after careful deliberation, I determined that it is in the national security interests of the United States to respond to the Assad regime's use of chemical weapons through a targeted military strike. The purpose of this strike would be to deter Assad from using chemical weapons, to degrade his regime's ability to use them, and to make clear to the world that we will not tolerate their use.[32]

In a speech about the decision to intervene in the Libyan insurgency of the Arab Spring, President Obama offered still more illuminating insight:

> It is true that America cannot use our military wherever repression occurs. And given the costs and risks of intervention, we must always measure our interests against the need for action. But that cannot be an argument for never acting on behalf of what's right. In this particular country - Libya; at this particular moment, we were faced with the prospect of violence on a horrific scale. We had a unique ability to stop that violence: an international mandate for action, a broad coalition prepared to join us, the support of Arab countries, and a plea for help from the Libyan people themselves. We also had the ability to stop Gaddafi's forces in their tracks without putting American troops on the ground.[33]

When considering these statements, a blueprint for informal critical input emerges. The Commander-in-Chief required information about four subjects: the presence of a mandate, popular opinion in the nation in question, the capability of the United States to affect the situation, and the risk incurred through action. Decision processes vary in different

---

[31]John Roberts, interview with MAJ Michael Fogarty, Colorado Springs, CO, March 20, 2014

[32]Barack Obama, "Remarks by the President in Address to the Nation On Syria" (speech, White House, Washington, DC, September 10, 2013), http://www.whitehouse.gov/the-press-office/2013/09/10/remarks-president-address-nation-syria (accessed October 5, 2013).

[33]Barack Obama, "Remarks by the President in Address to the Nation on Libya" (speech, National Defense University, Washington, DC, March 28, 2011), http://www.whitehouse.gov/the-press-office/2011/03/28/remarks-president-address-nation-libya (accessed October 5, 2013).

administrations and departments, but these criteria provide a sound basis for continued investigation.

According to the United States National Security Strategy, the decision to use military force in any case consists of a calculation of the costs of action as compared to the costs of inaction.[34] The essence lies in tabulating those costs. This study asserts that the best measure available is the determination of critical decision inputs through formal and informal indicators. It will therefore evaluate the frameworks in question by their utility in illuminating national interest, mandate, popular will, capability to act, and risk.

Phenomenon of Insurgency

This study asserts that insurgency theory must inform this process in three ways. First, it must help build understanding of the beginning of insurgency. The operative question is why. Why do insurgencies develop? This question gets to the root causes of insurgency. Second, insurgency theory must enhance understanding of how insurgencies operate to achieve their goals. The question here is how. Knowing more about how insurgencies operate unlocks clues concerning the mechanics and rise and fall of movements. Finally, theory should inform understanding of how insurgencies end. The most relevant question here may be: then what. What leads to ultimate success or failure? Knowing more about the phenomenon of insurgency insures that sound criteria figure into the evaluation of the assessment frameworks.

Roots of Insurgency - Why?

Many brilliant minds have attempted to demystify the root causes of insurgency and revolt. Hypotheses proliferate and some resonance exists on certain issues, but consensus and certainty prove elusive. This effort is not new. Karl Marx and Friedrich Engels based the ideology of socialism on the theoretical construct that capitalism contained within its structure the seeds of

---

[34]Obama, *National Security Strategy: May 2010,* 17.

18

its own demise. Vladimir Lenin, and Mao Zedong after him, would adapt Marxist principles to their unique realities. This theoretical tradition midwifed many insurgencies in the 20th century that author Bard O'Neill collectively describes as "Egalitarian" insurgencies.[35] Successors added unique contributions. For example, while he affirmed the concepts of people's war, Che Guevara suggested that the conditions for revolution need not be completely fulfilled; the revolution would accomplish that.[36] He caveats that statement by acknowledging that a state that maintains at least the "appearance of constitutional legality" will prove inhospitable to guerrilla warfare. David Kilcullen advanced an argument along similar lines. He suggested that violent extremists generate new recruits through a process of infection, contagion, intervention, and rejection.[37] Simply put, by inserting themselves into the environment, insurgents enable further development of their organization through provocative activities. Misagh Parsa postulated that exclusive polities and state hyperactivity lead to a greater likelihood of revolution. He further speculated that opportunities, organizations, mobilization options, coalition formulation and disruptions in social structure further aid in explaining the outbreak of revolution. All of these theoretical constructs are useful, but with the exception of Marx, they primarily explain the growth of insurgencies; the worsening of the problem, so to speak.

There is a more fundamental level of insurgency. What provides the initial spark of grievance? What factor plants the ideological seed? Ted Robert Gurr's *Why Men Rebel* remains one of the most durable and influential examinations of this underlying compulsion. He hypothesized:

> The potential for collective violence varies strongly with the intensity and scope of relative deprivation among members of a collectivity. Relative Deprivation (RD) is

---

[35]Bard E. O'Neill, *Insurgency and Terrorism: from Revolution to Apocalypse*, 2nd ed. (Washington, DC: Potomac Books Inc., 2005), 20.

[36]Che Guevara, *Guerrilla Warfare* (Lincoln: University of Nebraska Press, 1985), 47.

[37]David Kilcullen, *The Accidental Guerrilla: Fighting Small Wars in the Midst of a Big One* (Oxford, UK: Oxford University Press, 2009), 35.

defined as actors' perception of discrepancy between their value expectations and their value capabilities. Value expectations are the goods and conditions of life to which people believe they are rightfully entitled. Value capabilities are the goods and conditions they think they are capable of getting and keeping.[38]

Gurr was not the first to use the term relative deprivation. The term belongs mainly to sociology. He brought the term into the study of conflict, violence, and insurgency. The simplicity and foundational nature of this explanation make it a good fit for this study. Relative deprivation will serve as the basis for one of the evaluation criteria for the study.

Mechanics of Insurgency - How?

Insurgents and counterinsurgents alike concern themselves with the mechanics of insurgency. Mao approached the subject with unprecedented depth and specificity. Among other contributions, he gave the field the basis for an insurgency life cycle model that is still in use today. Part theorist and part strategist, Mao's theories continue to influence many practitioners to this day. Also part theorist and part strategist, Che Guevara used his experience in the Cuban revolution to instruct followers on how to employ the FOCO, or military/guerrilla focused strategy. Carlos Marighella described the mechanics of urban-based insurgency in the *Minimanual of the Urban Guerrilla*. In the two latter cases, however, the dominant focus is on employing tactics and strategy. Pure theory derives mainly from other sources, such as Mao, and receives short shrift.

Although it channels many other original theorists, Bard O'Neill's *Insurgency &Terrorism* effectively summarizes many resonant elements of the mechanics of insurgency. In particular, three elements stand out. First, O'Neill identifies the need to understand what type of insurgency is taking place in order to better understand the end state modus operandi of the group or groups. He identifies nine categories of insurgency with varying goals: anarchist, egalitarian, traditionalist, pluralist, apocalyptic-utopian, secessionist, reformist, preservationist, and

---

[38]Ted Robert Gurr, *Why Men Rebel* (Princeton, NJ: Princeton University Press, 1970), 24.

commercialist.[39] Second, he describes the importance of understanding the movement's strategy.

He lays out four main strategies used by insurgents: conspiratorial, protracted popular war,

military-focus, and urban-warfare.[40] Finally, though he defines it as belonging to the protracted

popular war strategy originally developed by Mao, O'Neill defines the three basic stages of

insurgency: strategic defensive, guerrilla warfare, and strategic offensive.[41] Together, the

category, strategy, and stage of an insurgency provide much context for an insurgency. For that

reason, these tools will be included as the basis for additional evaluation criteria.

End States of Insurgency - Then What?

The concept of end state in insurgency carries weight with this study. Knowing how

insurgencies eventually succeed or fail influences the study of the phenomenon. Many theorists

consider the concept of end game in some form or fashion. In his iconic *War of the Flea*, Robert

Taber uses the extended metaphor of a dog afflicted by fleas to explain common insurgent

theories of victory. In short, the ubiquitous insurgent (flea) wins by causing anemia. The large

and unwieldy government (dog) becomes overextended, unpopular, and bankrupt.[42] In *The Logic*

of Violence in Civil War, Stathis Kalyvas lays out a theory of irregular war that takes a different

angle on end games. He begins with an assumption that he shares with many contemporaries, that

"it is enough to assume, following Tilly (1978:201), that launching an insurgency and eventually

winning requires only 'the commitment of a significant part of the population, regardless of

motives, to exclusive alternative claims to control over the government currently exerted by the

members of the polity.'"[43] From there, he elaborates his theory, whereby a party to a conflict

---

[39]O'Neill, 20.

[40]Ibid, 46.

[41]Ibid, 50.

[42]Robert Taber, *The War of the Flea* (New York, NY: Lyle Stuart, 1965), 28.

[43]Stathis N. Kalyvas, *The Logic of Violence in Civil War*, Cambridge Studies in Comparative Politics (Cambridge, UK: Cambridge University Press, 2006), 101.

establishes their eventual sovereignty through the self-reinforcing phenomena of collaboration and control. Of these, control supersedes collaboration in the hierarchy.[44]

The RAND Corporation took a more pragmatic approach to end states. Ben Connable and Martin Libicki authored a report, *How Insurgencies End*, to provide empirical evidence to corroborate theories of victory and defeat. Their findings generally concur with the state of the art in insurgency thinking. Among their main conclusions they point out that "With a few exceptions, lasting insurgency endings are shaped not by military action but by social, economic, and political change."[45] Additional findings include the importance of external support, sanctuary, attention to root causes and grievances, and the ability to extend control over the population. Population control here correlates closely to Kalyvas' conception. The RAND study proves especially compelling because of its emphasis on empiricism and value to the practitioner, matters that are at the heart of *this* study. Connable and Libicki accept that their unique blend of qualitative and quantitative analysis does not allow for fundamental conclusions, but the weight of circumstantial evidence demands attention. Therefore, this study will utilize the aforementioned RAND conclusions - external support, sanctuary, redress of grievances, population control - as evaluation criteria for the assessment methodologies. The degree to which a methodology accounts for these four qualities will equate to its evaluation.

---

[44]Kalyvas, 145.

[45]Ben Connable and Martin C. Libicki, *How Insurgencies End* (Santa Monica, CA: RAND Corporation, 2010), 154.

METHODOLOGY

In order to provide an evaluation of the three assessments in question, this monograph will apply each assessment to a series of cases and then review the outputs generated to determine effectiveness. To do this, three steps must be performed. The first step in this process is to select and justify case studies of insurgencies selected for use in this study. The second step will then apply the individual assessments to each case study in turn. The final step will evaluate the effectiveness of each assessment tool by comparing the outputs generated to the decision making requirements first raised in the introduction.

Case Studies

The selection of useful case studies poses a significant challenge. The long history of insurgency and the multitude of examples hint at the difficulty of this task. The scope of this study requires realistic focus. It must therefore limit the case pool to the fewest number that can adequately represent the phenomenon of insurgency that the United States faces in the current environment. This process of limitation must address three factors: time, setting, and intensity. Because the study intends to address conflicts in the present and future, it will not consider insurgencies that have already concluded. Choosing contemporary examples ensures that questions of time and currency do not interfere with the intended purpose. On the question of intensity, cases selected will consist of points along a spectrum. The cases cannot reflect every size and shape of insurgency, but a sample provides a more useful test of the targeted assessment frameworks than a set of like examples. The approach to setting requires greater discretion. Owing to the vast array of variables that contribute to the setting of an insurgency - language, religion, geography, ethnicity, development, and culture to name only a few - this study elects to focus on a single region. This choice clearly offers advantages. By choosing multiple cases from within the same region, the process controls some of the inherent tendency for selection bias. It also limits the interference of external variables that sidetrack the most useful pieces of the analysis. The drawbacks of this approach are equally clear. The analysis sacrifices breadth for depth and does not allow for a comparison of how the chosen frameworks would perform in different regions. In summary, the selection of cases from within the same region aids the analysis of the assessments, but it also presents a clear limitation to the study.

This study focuses on cases of insurgency in the Trans-Sahel region of Africa. The region exhibits numerous ongoing conflicts and therefore presents fertile ground for analysis. Many insurgencies currently rage in the area. Of these, three have been selected to provide a viable cross section: Boko Haram of Nigeria, the Movement for the Emancipation of the Niger Delta of Nigeria, and the National Movement for the Liberation of Azawad of Mali. Each represents a discrete ongoing movement that meets the definition of an insurgency. This study uses Bard O'Neill's definition of insurgency:

> Insurgency may be defined as a struggle between a nonruling group and the ruling authorities in which the nonruling group consciously uses *political resources* (e.g. organizational expertise, propaganda, and demonstrations) and *violence* to destroy, reformulate, or sustain the basis of legitimacy of one or more aspects of politics.[46]

This definition serves as the foundation for the concept.

Assessment Application

The study will apply the assessment frameworks to the case studies in a straightforward fashion. Each framework will analyze each case. For example, the ICAF will first be applied to Boko Haram. Next it will be applied to the Movement for the Emancipation of the Niger Delta and the National Movement for the Liberation of Azawad in turn. Then the Guide for the Analysis of Insurgency will be applied. Finally, the Army Design Methodology will be applied to all three cases in the same fashion. In total, this process will feature nine separate summaries of the analyses. Due to considerations for length, the study will analyze each case fully but present

---

[46]O'Neill, 15.

only the findings. The analysis of each framework will address any specific challenges that it presents within the body of that section.

Assessment Evaluation

Two lines of criteria contribute to an overall evaluation of the three frameworks. The first line of criteria consists of policymaker decision criteria. It attempts to capture the expressed information preferences of policymakers who are faced with decisions to intervene in insurgencies. A sound assessment methodology should contribute to the understanding of the consumer and effectively satisfy information requirements. Per the previous chapter, the five factors that an insurgency assessment should address are the national interest, mandate, popular will, capability to act, and risk. These are the evaluation criteria for policymaker decision utility. Each assessment will receive a mark based on how effectively they account for these factors: high, low, or not applicable.

The second line of criteria consists of factors defining the phenomenon of insurgency. It seeks to capture factors spanning the continuum of insurgency: root causes of insurgency - why, mechanics of insurgency - how, and insurgency end states -then what. A sound assessment methodology should effectively grasp the phenomenon of insurgency. Again, per the previous chapter the evaluation criteria established are recognition of relative deprivation, category of insurgency, insurgent strategy, life cycle stage, external support, sanctuary, redress of grievances, and population control. Each methodology will likewise be evaluated by its effectiveness in accounting for these factors. Having compiled these evaluations, the final portion of the study presents conclusions about the overall utility of the methodologies and formulates relevant recommendations.

The recent past vividly demonstrated the consequences of failing to address adequately the dangers posed by insurgencies and failing states. Terrorist networks can find sanctuary within the borders of a weak nation and strength within the chaos of social breakdown. A nuclear-armed state could collapse into chaos and criminality. The most likely catastrophic threats to the U.S. homeland -- for example, that of a U.S. city being poisoned or reduced to rubble by a terrorist attack -- are more likely to emanate from failing states than from aggressor states..

—Secretary Robert Gates

ANALYSIS

This section will apply each of the chosen frameworks to each of the insurgency case studies. Each framework section will begin with an overview of how the methodology works. It will then apply the methodology first to Boko Haram, then the Movement for the Emancipation of the Niger Delta, and finally the National Movement for the Liberation of Azawad. The Interagency Conflict Assessment Framework will be applied first, followed by the Guide for the Analysis of Insurgency, and the Army Design Methodology.

Case Analysis

Boko Haram - Nigeria

The name Boko Haram is shorthand for its complete name: Jama'atu Ahl as-Sunnah li-Da'awati wal-Jihad, or Group of the Sunni People for the Calling and Jihad. Boko Haram derives from a colloquial translation of "western education forbidden". Experts say the group supports an Islamic state, complete with an Islam-centered education and Sharia law.[47] These issues are not new within Nigeria. The roots of political Islam date back to the 11th century with the conversion of the Borno Kingdom located in modern day Northeastern Nigeria.[48] The marriage of law and religion persisted into the colonial era, which began at the turn of the 20th century. Throughout the colonial period in Nigeria the British relied heavily upon local rule, including Sharia law in

---

[47]Mohammed Aly Sergie and Toni Johnson, *Boko Haram: Backgrounder* (New York: Council on Foreign Relations, 2014), http://www.cfr.org/nigeria/boko-haram/p25739 (accessed November 28, 2013).

[48]*Northern Nigeria: Background to Conflict* (Washington, DC: International Crisis Group, 2010), 3, http://www.crisisgroup.org/~/media/Files/africa/west-africa/nigeria/168%20Northern%20Nigeria%20-%20Background%20to%20Conflict.pdf (accessed January 15, 2014).

parts of the North.[49] The second half of the 20th century, which encompassed the latter years of colonial rule, the first republic, and the years of military rule, saw a demotion of Sharia law to jurisdiction of personal and religious matters. In 1999, coinciding with the end of military rule, 12 Northern states re-established Sharia on a limited basis. Struggles with implementation led to tension and uprising. Combined with longstanding scar tissue over the ascendance of Western education, corruption, and security force opacity, this tension contributed to the founding of the Boko Haram movement under the leadership of Mohammed Yusuf in 2002. A faction of the group became known colloquially as the Nigerian Taliban, a title it received from unsupportive local citizens living near the group's base.[50] After a series of clashes with government forces in 2003-04, the group favored distancing itself non-violently from government control. That trend continued until 2009, when heavy handed responses by the Nigerian Police Force resulted in the death of Mohammed Yusuf and many other of its members. From that point, violence escalated consistently.

Few analysts hazard a guess at Boko Haram's exact strength. The Africa Center for Strategic Studies reports the number of active militants in the "low hundreds" with additional supporters numbering perhaps "a few thousand".[51] The movement entered its most militant phase in 2009, and the volume of attacks has increased steadily since. Since 2010, Boko Haram claims as many attacks as all other Nigerian militant groups combined.[52] Activity originated in the upper northeast of the country and crept further west and south into the heartland of the country progressively. These attacks trend toward greater sophistication in addition to greater range. The

---

[49]*Northern Nigeria: Background to Conflict*, 4.

[50]J. Peter Pham, *Africa Security Brief: Boko Haram's Evolving Threat* (Washington, DC: Africa Center for Strategic Studies, 2012), 2, http://africacenter.org/wp-content/uploads/2012/04/AfricaBriefFinal_20.pdf (accessed March 8, 2014).

[51]Ibid.

[52]James Forest, *Confronting the Terrorism of Boko Haram in Nigeria* (Tampa, FL: Joint Special Operations University, 2012), 65.

vast majority of attacks follow two simple modus operandi: armed attacks with crude weapons or small arms, and improvised bombings. Many of these attacks were simple drive-by shootings or improvised grenade attacks. In 2011, Boko Haram launched the first suicide bombing attack in Nigerian history, an attack on the Nigerian Police Headquarters in Abuja that killed six. In August of that year, it conducted a still more sophisticated and deadly attack by bombing the United Nations building in the secure diplomatic district of Abuja. A vehicle-borne improvised explosive device detonated (as in the case of the Police Headquarters) killing twenty-three.[53] Analysts point to a probable link to Al Qaeda in the Islamic Maghreb and Al Shabaab to help explain the growing capability of Boko Haram.[54]

Boko Haram seeks purification of a state that it views as tainted. The secularity of law and the state form the cornerstone of the group's disaffection. Views that the Christians dominated the government in Abuja and aligned themselves too closely with the West fueled tensions.[55] Interestingly, other core grievances converge notably with other movements in Nigeria with differing ideological bases. These grievances include corruption, economic inequality, and security force abuses.[56] Infrastructure proliferates in the oil rich south, and along with it, the opportunity for economic advancement. Poverty rates run two to three times higher in the North than in the South and the Delta region.[57] Corruption pervades all of Nigeria. In his book *A Culture of Corruption*, Daniel Jordan Smith probes the depth of the problem: "Nigeria's international identity is so intertwined with its reputation for corruption that it is no wonder that the skills required to execute some forms of corruption are occasionally the object of popular

---

[53]Forest, 69.

[54]Ibid, 78.

[55]Ibid, 63.

[56]Pham, 7.

[57]Sergie and Johnson.

admiration."[58] Finally, security force abuses undermine sensibilities of justice. Amnesty International charges that the Nigerian Police Force is responsible for hundreds of extrajudicial killings and enforced disappearances every year, and few are investigated.[59] These abuses affect all Nigerians, but members of Boko Haram have an especially acute awareness of the problem. Their former leader, Mohammed Yusuf, was killed in 2009 by police while in custody, a fact that contradicted an earlier story by police officials.[60] Amid these deep ideological divides and serious social problems, Boko Haram continues to find support.

Boko Haram envisions Islam as the means for a more just and virtuous nation. A state based upon the Koran and Islamic law remains the group's desired end state. This study assesses the group to be a traditionalist insurgency in Bard O'Neill's typology. The dominant views expressed include a return to religious and moral standards of an imagined bygone era. Alternate possibilities can be constructed. The potential seems to exist within the group for a growing secessionist bent. This trajectory might resemble that of the Sudanese People's Liberation Army, which began its movement as a reformist insurgency, and ended in secession and separate statehood. In the present day, there is evidence that Boko Haram seeks to cause instability, insecurity, and sectarian violence within the populace.[61] Degradation of security tends to favor strict and well organized Islamic militias, as in the cases of Taliban-era Afghanistan and Mali during the most recent crisis. Should the capacity of the state wane far enough, the opportunity might present itself for Boko Haram to seize power by force. A nationwide legislative victory appears unlikely.

---

[58]Daniel Jordan Smith, A Culture of Corruption: Everyday Deception and Popular Discontent in Nigeria (Princeton: Princeton University Press, 2007), 221.

[59]Killing at Will: Extrajudicial Executions and Other Unlawful Killings by the Police In (London, UK: Amnesty International, 2009), 1, http://www.amnesty.org/en/library/asset/AFR44/038/2009/en/f09b1c15-77b4-40aa-a608-b3b01bde0fc5/afr440382009en.pdf (accessed January 6, 2014).

[60]Forest, 64.

[61]Ibid, 65.

Movement for the Emancipation of the Niger Delta - Nigeria

The Movement for the Emancipation of the Niger Delta (MEND) emerged onto the international scene in 2006 after the capture of foreign oil workers operating in Nigeria. The group seeks to reverse the pattern of environmental degradation of the Delta and the misappropriation of the nation's oil revenue.[62] The area knew a series of violent cycles before Nigeria's 1960 independence. These cycles related primarily to slavery and rivalry over palm oil production.[63] After independence, unrest shifted to the politics of petroleum production, but underdevelopment and lack of economic opportunity remained a potent undercurrent. In particular, two previous rebellions built a legacy of conflict in the Delta: Isaac Boro's "Twelve Day Revolution" and the Movement for the Survival of the Ogoni People (MOSOP).[64] Boro's revolt in 1966 sought to establish an independent "Niger Delta People's Republic" and control the rights to the region's resources by requiring oil companies to negotiate with his faction. The revolt was put down by the government with suspected resourcing help from Shell Oil.[65] In 1990, the MOSOP, under the leadership of Ken Saro-Wiwa, organized to empower the Ogoni people in the Delta Region politically and economically. The group demonstrated the ability to assemble 250,000 supporters at one time at a rally in 1993.[66] Shell cited tensions in the region and shut down production in the area. The Nigerian Government cracked down on the movement, executing Saro-Wiwa and eight others for their alleged role in the murder of four MOSOP government collaborators. A third, more recent, movement, the Niger Delta People's Volunteer

---

[62]Stephanie Hanson, *MEND* (Council on Foreign Relations, 2007), http://www.cfr.org/nigeria/mend-niger-deltas-umbrella-militant-group/p12920 (accessed November 21, 2013).

[63]*Northern Nigeria: Background to Conflict*, 3.

[64]Ibid, 4.

[65]Ibid.

[66]Ibid, 5.

Force (NDPVF), emerged in 2004; this group is now difficult to distinguish from MEND, which appears to be a stronger and more broad based manifestation of the unrest the NDPVF started.[67]

Estimates of the group's strength vary from the low hundreds to the low thousands. Some experts suggest that MEND does not possess an integrated command structure, but rather serves as an ideological umbrella for smaller factions operating in a similar fashion.[68] Members claim allegiance alternately to MEND and other groups, obscuring the true nature of the groups, but perhaps enhancing their own operational flexibility. The inaugural attack took place in January 2006 with the taking of four foreign oil workers as hostages.[69] Thereafter, hostage taking continues as a significant part of the group's *modus operandi*. Other significant activities include attacks on oil pipelines and infrastructure. A sea change occurred in the conflict in 2009 when the government brokered an amnesty with MEND leaders.[70] Nevertheless, attacks have continued. The group's most spectacular attack was its bombing attack on Abuja in 2010. Two bombs killed twelve and injured seventeen at an Independence Day celebration in the capitol.[71] Despite President Goodluck Jonathan's denial that the attack was conducted by MEND, evidence pointed to the group. Eventually, South African authorities arrested and convicted Henry Okah, a MEND leader, of complicity in the attack. Likewise, incidences of attack on oil infrastructure continue, along with hostage taking and theft of oil.

Several commonalities exist between the grievances of MEND and those of Boko Haram. Corruption within the government and the oil sector weighs heavily in the critiques of both

---

[67]Hanson.

[68]*The Swamps of Insurgency: Nigeria's Delta Unrest*. International Crisis Group, 2006. http://www.crisisgroup.org/en/regions/africa/west-africa/nigeria/115-the-swamps-of-insurgency-nigerias-delta-unrest.aspx (accessed November 21, 2013).

[69]Hanson.

[70]Caroline Duffield, "Will Amnesty Bring Peace to Niger Delta?," *BBC News*, October 5, 2009, http://news.bbc.co.uk/2/hi/africa/8291336.stm (accessed December 1, 2013).

[71]"UK Vips Pulled Out Ahead of Deadly Nigeria Parade," *BBC News*, October 2, 2010, http://www.bbc.co.uk/news/world-africa-11458674 (accessed December 5, 2013).

groups. Both also cite heavy handed tactics by security forces. Additionally, the lack of economic development and the sense of being left behind amid Nigeria's rapid growth pervades both grievance narratives. Key differences exist also. MEND generally omits religious issues from its agenda. A recent and notable exception was the group spokesperson's warning of attacks against Islamic targets if attacks against Northern Nigerian churches continued.[72] Most importantly, MEND's dominant focus on the oil industry places it in a unique category. Economic opportunity and corruption figure significantly, but a major environmental component is also resident within this grievance. This component plays on two levels: oil production fouled the natural beauty and health of the ecosystem, and the destruction of habitat led to declining fish populations and income for fishermen. In the final analysis, however, MEND's grievances center on resource control.[73]

MEND functions as a reformist insurgency. The distribution of resources within the existing regime trumps other goals. The rhetoric focuses on justice within the existing system and redress for grievances rather than overturning the existing social order. Some analysts argue that MEND aims to set the agenda, make oil exploitation progressively more unprofitable, and thereby compel a political settlement granting it a fair stake in oil revenue and potentially greater political representation.[74]

---

[72]Shaji Matthew and Chris Kay, "Nigeria's Mend Issues Threat to Bomb Mosques, Kill Clerics," *Bloomberg News*, April 15, 2013, accessed December 5, 2013, http://www.bloomberg.com/news/2013-04-15/nigeria-s-mend-issues-threat-to-bomb-mosques-kill-clerics-2-.html (accessed February 1, 2014).

[73]Hanson.

[74]Ibid.

National Movement for the Liberation of Azawad - Mali

The National Movement for the Liberation of Azawad (MNLA)[75] represents the most

consistent insurgent movement in recent Malian history. The group seeks to establish an

independent state for ethnic Tuareg people. The would-be nation of Azawad consists of Tuareg

populated lands in Northern Mali, Northern Burkina Faso and Southern Algeria.[76] The people,

originally known among their own as Imouchar, received the name Tuareg from rival Arab

tribes.[77] They relate ethnically to the Berbers of Northern Africa, but diverge in language, aspects

of their brand of Islam, and their pastoral nomadic culture.[78] There have been four major periods

of Tuareg unrest since independence in 1960. The first raged from 1962-64 before being

suppressed by the young Malian government. The second took place in the early 1990s, roughly

covering the years 1990-96.[79] The third period stretched from 2006-09. The fourth and final

period began in early 2012, and ended in January 2013 with French intervention restoring the

Malian government's control over the preponderance of its territory. During all three of the most

recent periods the MNLA proved to be the most important single actor. It served as the catalyst

for Tuareg discontent and rebellion and as a hot house for unreconciled factions.[80] The 2012 crisis

represented the most complex challenge to the government of Mali. It began as another Tuareg

rebellion, relatively small in size, but continued to evolve. The unique features of this revolt were

a concurrent military coup in Bamako and the alliance of the MNLA to Islamist militants who

---

[75]MNLA stands for the Movement National pour la Liberation d'Azawad; this name is
transliterated to the National Movement for the Liberation for the purpose of this study, but the original
acronym is retained to maintain consistency with much of the literature.

[76]Kalifa Keita "Conflict and Conflict Resolution in the Sahel: The Tuareg Insurgency in Mali"
(master's thesis, U.S. Army War College, 1998), 9.

[77]Dugald Campbell, *On the Trail of the Veiled Tuareg* (London, UK: Seeley, Service and
Company, 1928), 19.

[78]Keita, 6.

[79]Angel Rabasa et al., *From Insurgency to Stability* (Santa Monica, CA: RAND Corporation,
2011), 123.

[80]Ibid, 125.

effectively co-opted the movement. These Militants included Al Qaeda in the Islamic Maghreb, Ansar ed-Dine, and at least three splinter factions of those groups. In effect, three separate crises interacted simultaneously: a political crisis brought on by the coup, a secessionist crisis brought on by the MNLA insurgency, and a terrorist crisis brought on by the activities of Islamist rebels.[81] Without timely intervention from France, the combined insurgent force may have taken the capital.

The 2012 insurgency started in much the same fashion as the previous three revolts. At the time, it counted as many as 10,000 fighters in its ranks.[82] MNLA rebels attacked outposts in Menaka, reigniting the conflict that had cooled just three years before.[83] In all four instances of major insurgent activity in Mali, groups initiated their struggle by targeting government and military outposts in the Tuareg populated North.[84] The lone exception to this took place in 2006 when a group of Tuareg military personnel calling themselves the Democratic Alliance for Change deserted and demanded dialogue without attacking.[85] The MNLA directed subsequent attacks at defeating government forces in the North. In April of 2012, the MNLA controlled Northern Mali and declared independence. Though the International Criminal Court opened a probe into the Mali situation generally, evidence of MNLA atrocities appears inconclusive thus

---

[81]David Francis, *The Regional Impact of the Armed Conflict and French Intervention in Mali* (Oslo, NO: Norwegian Peacebuilding Resource Centre, 2013), 2, http://www.peacebuilding.no/var/ezflow_site/storage/original/application/f18726c3338e39049bd4d554d4a22c36.pdf (accessed March 14, 2014).

[82]*Situation in Mali: Article 53(1) Report* (The Hague, NL: International Criminal Court, 2013), 18, http://www.icc-cpi.int/en_menus/icc/situations%20and%20cases/situations/icc0112/Documents/SASMaliArticle53_1PublicReportENG16Jan2013.pdf (accessed January 2, 2014).

[83]Richard Valdmanis, "Tuareg Fighters Attack Town in Northern Mali," *Reuters*, January 17, 2012, http://www.reuters.com/article/2012/01/17/us-mali-attack-idUSTRE80G0YH20120117 (accessed February 5, 2014).

[84]Keita, 10.

[85]Rabasa et al., 124.

far.[86] Here the case of Ansar ed-Dine bears some scrutiny. It formed under the former MNLA leader Iyad Ag Ghaly when that group rebuffed his attempts to lead.[87] Working with Al Qaeda in the Islamic Maghreb, the group turned on its erstwhile ally, the MNLA, and hijacked the gains of the rebellion, a now archetypal Al Qaeda political strategy.[88] International investigators primarily attribute terrorist activities and crimes against the populace to Al Qaeda in the Islamic Maghreb and Ansar ed-Dine, but the MNLA may have participated in the killing of between 70 and 153 detained Malian soldiers at Aguelhuk.[89]

The Tuareg MNLA (along with some Arab parties in the area) seeks an independent homeland as a guarantee of autonomy. The pattern throughout the 20th century consisted of Tuareg revolt based on root causes of lost autonomy and economic insecurity followed by Government responses of repression mixed with reconciliation. With French colonial administrations and post-independence governments alike, the Tuareg experienced friction with their way of life. They chafed at a two-fold loss of autonomy: first owing to the encroachment of modernity on their traditional and pastoral way of life, second due to domination from the South.[90] Other factors no doubt contributed to the latest round of insurgent activity. Analysts suspect that the MNLA received an influx of fighters and weapons from Libya after that country's civil war. These fighters probably originally hailed from Mali but left to fight under Qaddafi in Libya some years prior.[91]

---

[86]*Situation in Mali: Article 53(1) Report*, 12.

[87]Steve Metcalf, "Iyad Ag Ghaly - Mali's Islamist Leader," *BBC News*, July 17, 2012, http://www.bbc.com/news/world-africa-18814291 (accessed January 16, 2014).

[88]"Mali Profile," *BBC News*, December 27, 2013, http://www.bbc.com/news/world-africa-13881978 (accessed January 15, 2014); Michael Clarke, *An Insight Into Jihadist Strategy in the Sahel* (London, UK: Royal United Services Institute, 2013), https://www.rusi.org/analysis/commentary/ref:C511D272D72DDC/#.UyO9MKm_k20 (accessed January 14, 2014).

[89]*Situation in Mali: Article 53(1) Report*, 21, 30.

[90]Keita, 9.

[91]Valdmanis.

Over the years, the MNLA theory of victory remains generally consistent: secession. Reformist strains occasionally hold sway, as in the case of the 2006 revolt, but secession lies at the heart of many of the rebellions. The rebels seek establishment of an independent Tuareg homeland that will be called Azawad. These revolts feature a strategy of gaining military control of much of Northern Mali. After an adequate level of control has been reached, the rebels will declare independence. The 2012 revolt proceeded almost exactly as such. The rebels achieved the final stage of insurgency, war of movement with the government. At that point, however, the conflict evolved. The harsh enforcement of political Islam and charges of terrorism by the MNLA's allies led to almost immediate outcry within Mali and in the International community. This, in turn, led to intervention by France. Should the MNLA choose to fight again, the choice to align with Islamist rebels may or may not recur. Connections to Al Qaeda in the Islamic Maghreb brought unwanted international attention and led to a deep rift in how to administer areas the insurgency controlled. The MNLA may work alone in future actions or may seek less polarizing allies to achieve the homeland it desires.

Application of Assessments

Interagency Conflict Assessment Framework - ICAF

The Interagency Conflict Assessment Framework follows a process with two basic tasks: conflict diagnosis, and segue to planning. The bulk of the analysis takes place during the first task. The second task provides a starting point to integrate into various other planning processes used by the interagency for detailed planning. The summaries that follow outline the results of applying ICAF to the insurgent case studies. Though large amounts of data, analysis, and synthesis underlay these summaries, they are necessarily truncated here. Additionally, this study used only task one from the ICAF. The rationale: the study describes phase zero assessments, and therefore, no mandate exists yet for intervention. Thus, the segue into planning would be an academic exercise which this study will not consider.

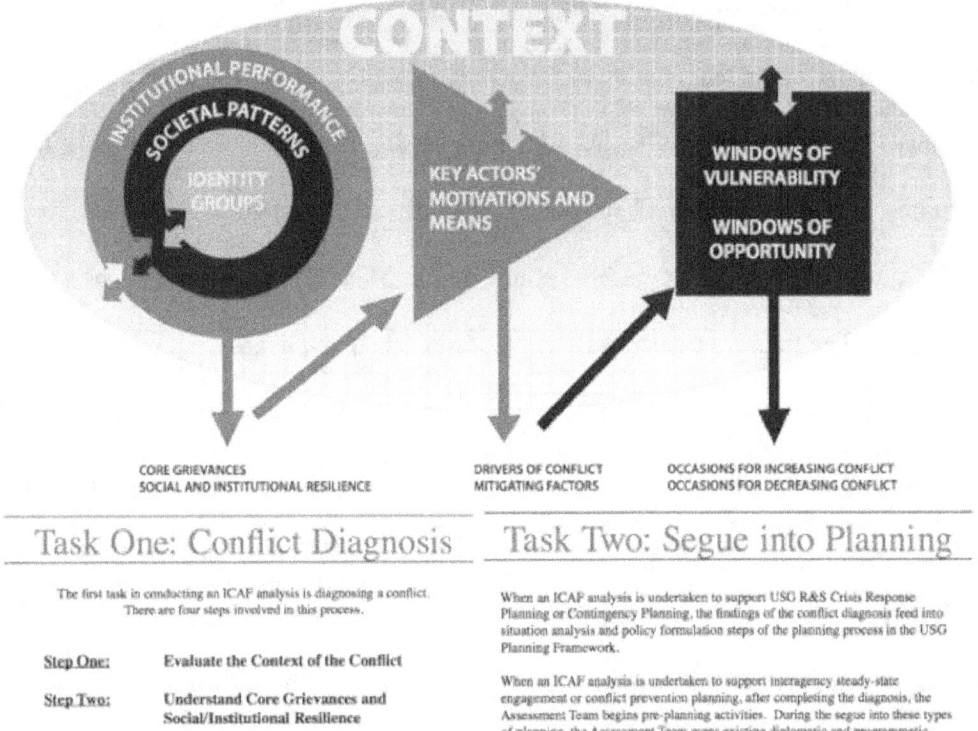

Figure 1: Interagency Conflict Assessment Framework Process Diagram

Source: United States Department of State, Office of the Coordinator for Reconstruction and Stabilization, *The Interagency Conflict Assessment Framework* (Washington, D.C.: S/CRS, 2008), 7.

ICAF - Boko Haram (BH)

Utilizing the ICAF to study the Boko Haram insurgency brought two key factors into focus. First, the importance of the issue of Islamic identity in Northern Nigeria became clear. The ICAF places a strong emphasis on the question of identity in assessments. Nigeria possesses a long history of political Islam. In the last one hundred years, however, governments from the colonial era, first republic, and the years of military rule espoused policies that crowded out the influence of Sharia law and Islamic education. In 1999, the government allowed for expanded Sharia in twelve Northern provinces, but tension persists. Devout Muslims in the North today believe that allowing the "Bokos" - loosely translated here as secular, pro-Western bureaucrats - to control policy led to the degradation of the North. Boko Haram taps into that disappointment and channels it into violent rebellion. Second, the opposing forces of cohesion and disintegration come to light. Dating back hundreds of years, people from diverse backgrounds have lived in relative harmony despite old religious and ethnic divides. The ICAF refers to this as a mitigating societal pattern. The framework also calls into question societal patterns that reinforce conflict. Interlocking issues of recent petroleum wealth and increasing corruption fall under this category. In a U.S. Army War College monograph, Gerald McLoughlin and Clarence Bouchat capture these forces succinctly, concluding that while "explosive growth of corruption may well hollow out the Nigerian state as it destroys the economic and political systems that support it....Long-standing cultural, historical, and economic ties still bind the country together."[92] Overall, the ICAF excels at providing insight into the shifting societal dynamics that drove Nigeria to the brink of crisis with the Boko Haram insurgency.

ICAF - Movement for the Emancipation of the Niger Delta (MEND)

As with the case study of Boko Haram, a key observation from the ICAF approach to MEND conflict is the importance of the identity question. Membership in this insurgency moves fluidly between groups. Leadership and goals remain ill-defined. This characteristic is instrumental in the flexibility of the organization, but it also represents a vulnerability. Members of an ethnic or tribal insurgency can only avoid conflict with great difficulty. Members can put aside ideological conflict as needed. This feature proves consequential in the case of MEND because identity issues present one of the key challenges in the conflict. Some experts suggest that MEND "is an idea more than an organization."[93] A second key takeaway from this

---

[92]Gerald McLoughlin and Clarence J. Bouchat, *Nigerian Unity: in the Balance* (Carlisle, PA: SSI, 2013), 64.

[93]Hanson.

assessment is that a successful campaign targeting the core grievances may find success in addressing this conflict. The mitigating factors analysis yields that the conflict remains largely bounded in economic and environmental issues. Though significant, these problems rank among the most solvable. This point relates to another significant outcome of this assessment. Task one, step four of the ICAF calls for the practitioner to examine windows of vulnerability (worsening) and windows of opportunity (improvement) within the conflict. With the offer of an amnesty period and temporary cease fire agreement in 2009, it appeared that the government was on the right track to wind down its conflict with MEND. Those actions opened a window. After that time, violence reignited. Analysts called the measures in play at that time insufficient to exploit that opportunity.[94] As a consequence, the window closed. Understanding the nature of those windows demonstrates some of the added value of the ICAF.

ICAF - National Movement for the Liberation of Azawad (MNLA)

Yet again, in the MNLA case, identity comes to the fore. As previously noted, the MNLA mainly consists of ethnic Tuaregs. The Tuareg have little in common with Southern Malians. The Tuareg are ethnically, linguistically, economically, and culturally distinct from Southerners. Since independence, this distinction led both parties to distrust one another. In the case of the Tuareg, they fear that the policies of a government dominated by Southern elites will continue to erode their pastoral and nomadic way of life. Those that try to integrate feel economically excluded by the lack of opportunities in the North. The sense that the Tuareg identity will die off drives much of the rebellious sentiment. Some believe that the Tuareg will only be free to pursue their way of life within an independent state - Azawad. The ICAF also sheds light upon the role institutional weakness plays in the persistence of conflict in Mali. This factor particularly helps to understand

---

[94]Xan Rice, "Nigeria Begins Amnesty for Niger Delta Militants," *Guardian*, August 6, 2009, http://www.theguardian.com/world/2009/aug/06/niger-delta-militants-amnesty-launched (accessed March 14, 2014).

the 2012 iteration of the conflict. At the outset, conflict raged within the government. The Army blamed the civil government for failing to adequately provide for defense. When another MNLA-led Tuareg insurgency appeared imminent, the Army took matters into its own hands by leading a coup. Perversely, this further weakened the state, and may have allowed the MNLA and its Islamist allies to make even more rapid gains. Even facing this grave threat, the government struggled to get a handle on the situation until the French entered the conflict. That long lasting moment of weakness within the government led to one of the aforementioned windows of vulnerability that the ICAF seeks to identify. This vulnerability proved especially devastating. Not only did it allow the MNLA to make rapid gains, but it opened the country up to malign influence from violent Islamist groups. These groups were in the process of executing a tried-and-true Al Qaeda strategy of hijacking existing political movements at moments of great vulnerability, therefore gaining disproportionate influence over the state of affairs.[95] Without timely intervention by the French, a radicalized insurgency may have swept the Malian government from power. The MNLA case study again shows that the ICAF methodology provides added value in diagnosing dynamic and oppositional forces in conflict prone areas.

Guide for the Analysis of Insurgency - GAI

The Guide for the Analysis of Insurgency focuses sharply on the phenomenon of insurgency. It captures the dynamics of insurgency successfully in a descriptive fashion. It does not purport to offer alternatives for action, but rather takes a snapshot of the situation at present. The GAI differs from the ICAF and the Army Design Methodology in its tendency toward detailed assessments rather than conceptual assessments. It seeks tangible data on the number of insurgents, their training, their supply, and the character of their propaganda.

---

[95]Michael Clarke, *An Insight Into Jihadist Strategy in the Sahel* (London, UK: Royal United Services Institute, 2013), https://www.rusi.org/analysis/commentary/ref:C511D272D72DDC/#.UyO9MKm_k20 (accessed January 14, 2014).

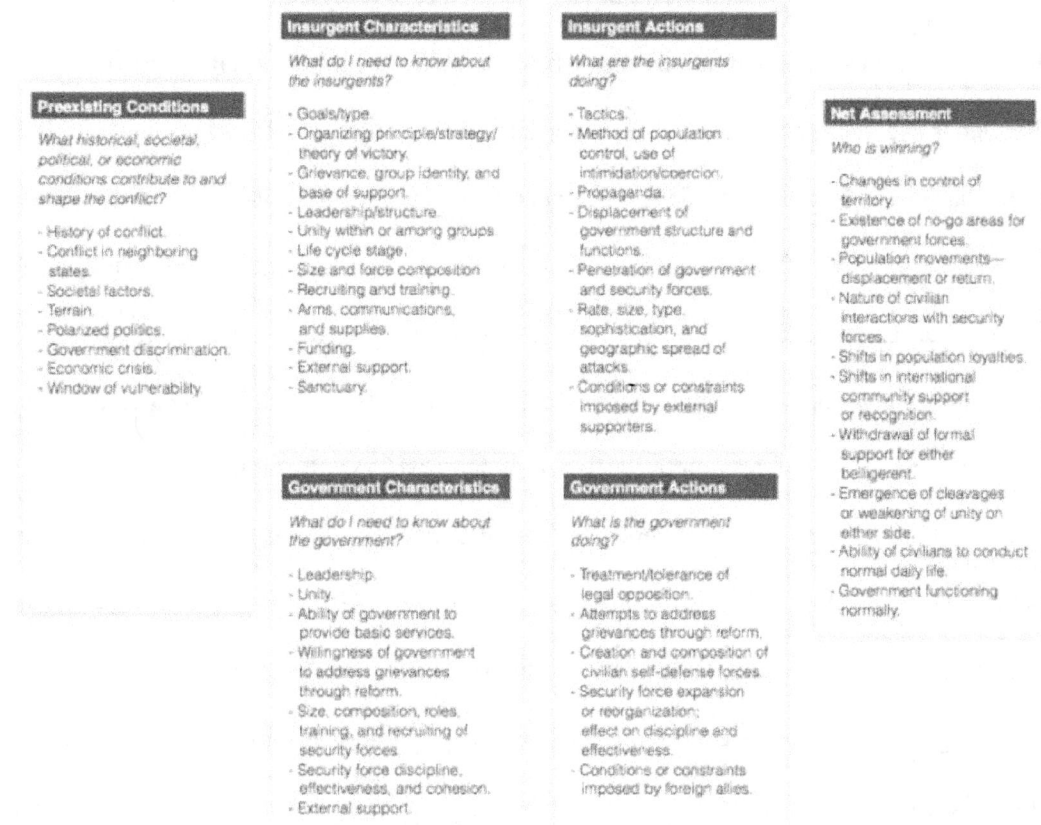

Preexisting Conditions

What historical, societal, political, or economic conditions contribute to and shape the conflict?

- History of conflict.
- Conflict in neighboring states.
- Societal factors.
- Terrain.
- Polarized politics.
- Government discrimination.
- Economic crisis.
- Window of vulnerability.

Insurgent Characteristics

What do I need to know about the insurgents?

- Goals/type.
- Organizing principle/strategy/theory of victory.
- Grievance, group identity, and base of support.
- Leadership/structure.
- Unity within or among groups.
- Life cycle stage.
- Size and force composition.
- Recruiting and training.
- Arms, communications, and supplies.
- Funding.
- External support.
- Sanctuary.

Insurgent Actions

What are the insurgents doing?

- Tactics.
- Method of population control, use of intimidation/coercion.
- Propaganda.
- Displacement of government structure and functions.
- Penetration of government and security forces.
- Rate, size, type, sophistication, and geographic spread of attacks.
- Conditions or constraints imposed by external supporters.

Government Characteristics

What do I need to know about the government?

- Leadership.
- Unity.
- Ability of government to provide basic services.
- Willingness of government to address grievances through reform.
- Size, composition, roles, training, and recruiting of security forces.
- Security force discipline, effectiveness, and cohesion.
- External support.

Government Actions

What is the government doing?

- Treatment/tolerance of legal opposition.
- Attempts to address grievances through reform.
- Creation and composition of civilian self-defense forces.
- Security force expansion or reorganization; effect on discipline and effectiveness.
- Conditions or constraints imposed by foreign allies.

Net Assessment

Who is winning?

- Changes in control of territory.
- Existence of no-go areas for government forces.
- Population movements—displacement or return.
- Nature of civilian interactions with security forces.
- Shifts in population loyalties.
- Shifts in international community support or recognition.
- Withdrawal of formal support for either belligerent.
- Emergence of cleavages or weakening of unity on either side.
- Ability of civilians to conduct normal daily life.
- Government functioning normally.

Figure 2: Guide for the Analysis of Insurgency Process Diagram

Source: U.S. Central Intelligence Agency, *Guide to the Analysis of Insurgency* (Washington, DC: Central Intelligence Agency, 2012), preface, https://www.hsdl.org/?view&did=713599 (accessed November 21, 2013).

GAI - Boko Haram (BH)

The character of the GAI quickly distinguishes itself from the ICAF when examining Boko Haram. The GAI focuses much more on the *how* questions behind an insurgency. The methodology asks the goals and type of the insurgency. Boko Haram represents a traditionalist insurgency. Militants lament the decline of society and advocate the return to some actual or perceived past glory. Boko Haram decries the corruption and moral degradation of Nigeria in the face of modernity. They seek a return to broader Sharia law and Islamic education that fell by the wayside generations earlier. The detailed and technical nature of the GAI also shows through in other ways. It specifically asks about funding. That subject may arise during assessments using the ICAF or Army Design Methodology, but the GAI makes it explicit. Analyzing Boko Haram's funding led to the observation that because it lacks a state sponsor, it relies on robbery, donations from the diaspora in Europe, the US, and Pakistan, and patronage from wealthy individuals within Nigeria. A probe of these wealthy individuals uncovered direct assistance from a sitting Member of Parliament to Boko Haram.[96] This analysis of details led to a re-examination of concepts. In this case, it suggests that national policy on the subject might be hampered or actively undermined by powerful individuals within the government. Another technical matter this methodology uses to judge insurgencies is the rate, size, type, sophistication, and geographic spread of attacks. For Boko Haram, the level of sophistication clearly rose in 2011 with its first suicide attack and its first attack in the capital, Abuja. These types of details may be most useful to a planning team considering employment of a specific operational approach. It seems less useful in the context of a phase zero assessment, except that it may reveal a benchmark of scope. The GAI assessment of Boko Haram differs significantly from the ICAF assessment, but the output appears at least as valuable.

GAI - Movement for the Emancipation of the Niger Delta (MEND)

Among the most important findings of the GAI assessment of MEND is the analysis of grievance, group identity, and base of support. These three factors correlate importantly in the study of insurgency. MEND mainly consists of tribal groups from the Niger Delta region: Ijaw and Ogoni, among others. Traditionally, many of these people fish for a living along the waterways of the Delta and earn their living from the fruits of the land. The rapid exploitation of oil resources in the Delta region led to significant environmental degradation. Consequently, fish populations, health, and quality of life degraded in turn. MEND's grievances concern the

---

[96]Forest, 71.

struggles of Delta people. They seek redress for environmental degradation, a greater share of oil wealth, improved economic opportunity for citizens of the area, and ways to hold the government accountable. The GAI also includes the all important consideration of strategy and theory of victory. MEND follows an indirect strategy that hints at its reformist nature. It primarily targets the oil industry: infrastructure, workforce, and enablers. It seeks to make oil exploitation progressively more difficult for the foreign oil companies that do most of the extraction. In so doing, those companies will in turn pressure the Nigerian government. Either the government must meet the demands of the movement or run the risk of losing its partner oil companies. As with many other questions, the GAI is the only methodology that explicitly asks the strategy and theory of victory of the belligerent. Knowledge of that aspect of an insurgency could prove crucially important in diagnosing its trajectory. Trajectory speaks to risk, and risk speaks volumes to policymakers.

GAI - National Movement for the Liberation of Azawad (MNLA)

The MNLA insurgency differs somewhat from MEND and Boko Haram examples. During the 2012 revolt, the MNLA controlled significant portions of Northern Mali. Alongside their Islamist allies, they established governance and administration mechanisms. Before setbacks at the hands of their former allies, they were in a much later stage of insurgency than the other two cases. For all their activities, Boko Haram and MEND remain in the latent and incipient stage of insurgency. In 2012, the MNLA progressed from that stage into guerrilla warfare, and then on into a war of movement with the government at a remarkable pace. The GAI assesses the life cycle stage of insurgency while other frameworks do not. The consideration of conflict in neighboring states that the GAI demands also proved especially influential to this assessment. Historical connections to Algeria and Libya played a major role in the most recent Mali conflict. Algeria has played a long standing and important role in past Mali conflicts owing to proximity, influence, and confluence of interests. Algeria also hosts one of the longest running Islamist

43

insurgencies in the region. AQIM played a major role in the 2012 conflict, but it originated as the Salafist Group for Preaching and Combat in Algeria. Libya does not share a border with Mali, but a large number of Tuareg fighters that formerly operated with Muammar Qaddafi returned to Mali after that country's civil war. This influx of fighters and weapons may have stimulated the urgency and feasibility of MNLA's rebellion at that time. Like the other case studies, studying the type of insurgency illuminates some tendencies of the MNLA. It tends to be a classic secessionist movement. The achievement of the state of Azawad is fundamental, but Azawad only includes traditional Tuareg areas. The government of Mali might recoil at that possibility, but the MNLA did not previously threaten the sovereignty of the South. That dynamic changed in 2012. The addition of aggressive Islamic militants disrupted the modus operandi of the MNLA and made the situation even more unpredictable. Another element of the GAI also adds to this analysis: conditions and constraints imposed by external support. Though not a state sponsor, Al Qaeda in the Islamic Maghreb and the quasi-indigenous Ansar ed-Dine originally provided assistance to the MNLA. Later, those organizations completely undermined the MNLA and changed the overall strategy in Mali. The GAI helps make that power dynamic clear.

Army Design Methodology - ADM

The Army Design Methodology is the Army's analytical multitool for complex environments and unstructured problems. It shows exceptional flexibility due to its endless capacity for tailoring. Wherever there is analytical flexibility there is risk. In this minimally structured approach, the risk exists that if the inputs chosen by the practitioner lack utility or accuracy, then the outputs will also share the same fate. The GAI provides a leading list of questions and topics for the investigator to address. ADM insists that the investigator author an original approach. This study uses the ADM in a somewhat unorthodox way. Instead of assuming the United States as the central actor, here the design reflects the insurgent's position. The operational approach is what would be required for the insurgent to achieve its desired end state.

This study takes this perspective because the planner can derive the insurgent's current state, end state, and problem with high confidence. On the other hand, the uncertain nature of US objectives during phase zero may not allow that level of confidence. Also, a phase zero insurgency assessment seeks to understand the nature of the movement. Employing the ADM from the insurgent perspective may therefore prove as valuable, if not more valuable, than employing it from an unclear US perspective.

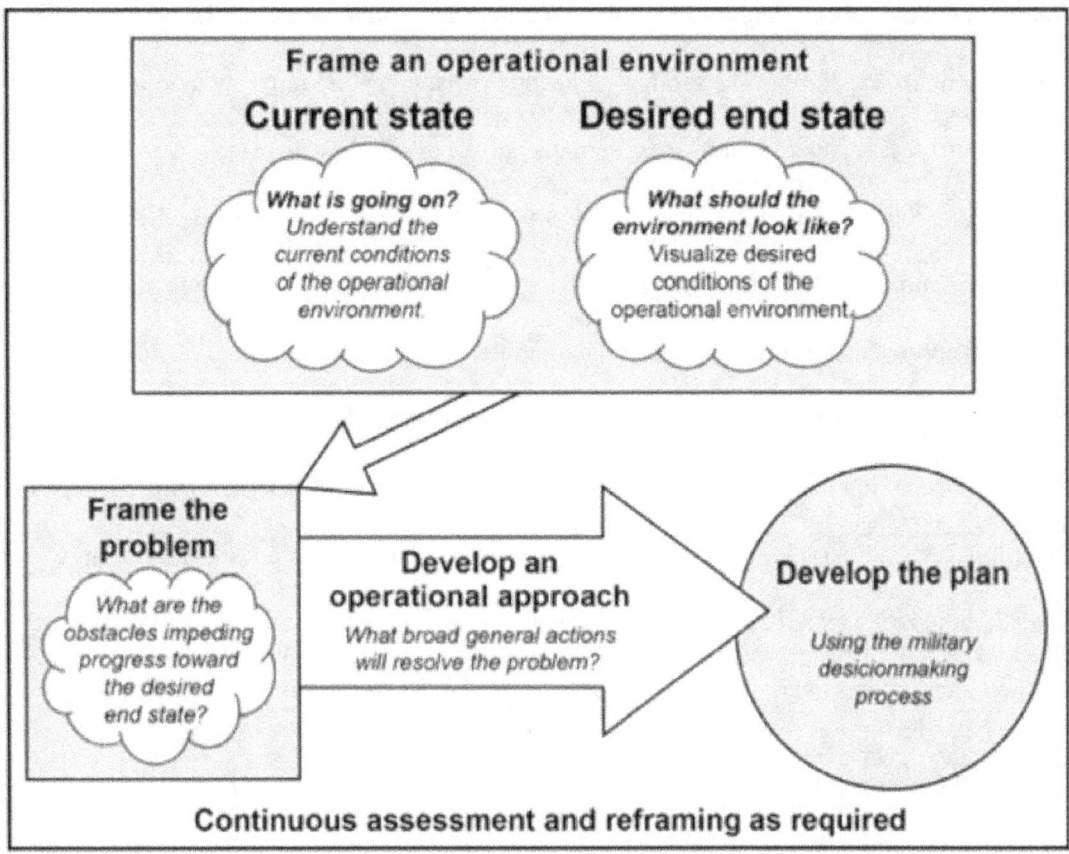

Figure 3: Army Design Methodology Process Diagram

Source: U.S. Army, Army Doctrine Reference Publication 5-0, The Operations Process, 143.

ADM - Boko Haram (BH)

The ADM excels at demonstrating how a belligerent party might evolve into the future. This contrasts with the GAI that largely captures a snapshot of the present moment. The ADM does this by projecting a potential operational approach. Clearly, when considering the future actions of an outside group, the practitioner must use a good deal of subjective judgment in making the link between the current situation, the nature of the problem, and the proposed operational approach. Use of subjective judgment exposes the assessment to risk. The opposite is also true. Unwillingness to use subjective judgment may also expose an assessment to the risk of being less useful. In the case of Boko Haram, the group's desired state of a regime that will expand Sharia law, favor Islamic education, and impose cultural change will likely require enhanced military capability. The group will need to expand beyond terrorism and intimidation into attacks to defeat government forces. Perhaps only then can they displace governance and impose a form they desire. This enhanced military capability places demands on the organization: more money, more weapons, training, new tactics, and better logistics. By anticipating the operational approach an insurgency may take, planners can better assess the trajectory of the conflict. This, again, speaks clearly to risk. Employing the ADM on the Boko Haram case also exposes an interesting constraint and potential. Generating the group's desired state of an Islamic regime founded on Sharia law begs the question: how much of Nigeria does Boko Haram wish to include? Should they experience success, if they broaden their effort to the West and South, they may encounter progressively stiffening resistance as they stray from their Islamic base of power. Therefore, their growth may be self-limiting.

ADM - Movement for the Emancipation of the Niger Delta (MEND)

Studying MEND with the ADM leads to a formulation of the insurgent strategy that appears very similar to the theory of victory uncovered by the GAI. MEND acts in an indirect fashion by applying pressure to the oil companies believing that those companies will then apply similar pressure to the Nigerian government. That pressure will then compel the government to address MEND's grievances. Though this output is roughly similar, the ADM offers an interesting insight as to why this strategy is necessary. The ADM includes a placeholder for conducting center of gravity analysis. One perspective of the center of gravity in the MEND case is that the Nigerian National Petroleum Company is the government's center of gravity. It allows for the generation of the vast majority of the government's revenue. This process shows the logic of targeting the petroleum economy in a different light. The ADM also differs somewhat in its portrayal of the broader context. ADM analysis revealed that Boko Haram represents an indirect factor in MEND conflict. The groups interact very little, outside of a threat MEND directed at Boko Haram after a series of attacks on Christians in the North.[97] Despite that fact, the Nigerian government's growing preoccupation with Boko Haram presents threats and opportunities to MEND as well. They can profit from that relationship, perhaps by avoiding further spectacular attacks and cultivating an image as a group that the government can work with in good faith. Continued preoccupation with Boko Haram might also prevent the government from bringing the desired amount of military force into the Delta region. In any case, contemplating Boko Haram's role helps put MEND's situation in context. The ADM generally does a good job of capturing those broad interactions.

ADM - National Movement for the Liberation of Azawad (MNLA)

The final case application considers the ADM's approach to the MNLA insurgency. After achieving a high water mark of success where it controlled much of Northern Mali and declared independence for Azawad, the MNLA finds itself knocked backward into the latent and incipient stage of insurgency. The ADM allows the practitioner to map out various tendencies and potentials of the MNLA's future. It must now contend with a regime that enjoys the direct support of a European military power for the immediate future. The potential of near term success appears slim. In spite of that fact, the government's unwillingness or inability to address the root causes of Tuareg unrest suggest that the tendency of recurring Tuareg revolt will continue. The

---

[97]Matthew and Kay.

potential, then, exists for a renewal of fighting after the MNLA reconstitutes its forces and awaits the slackening of the security situation in the North. The problem frame of the ADM demonstrates how obstacles preventing the group's success coalesce into a dominant, overarching problem. In the case of the MNLA, it must reconstitute its capabilities, isolate itself from the malign influence of Islamist groups, and build the legitimacy of an independent Azawad in order to gain the persistent relative superiority that they require over government forces in the North. Understanding this root problem helps clarify the MNLA's goals and objectives moving forward. Owing to their degraded state after the 2012 conflict, the reconstitution of capability takes priority in the near term. Eventually, however, the MNLA must gain adequate buy-in for its Azawad agenda or face additional outside interventions. The ADM makes this clear by generating a thread to follow from the current state, through the obstacles, and onto a potential path to the desired state. In short, the ADM helps us create a narrative to explain the arc of the conflict.

Evaluation

The evaluation of approaches represents the key to this study. Knowing where assessment methodologies' strengths and weakness lie enables practitioners to choose the right tool for the job. To review, the criteria selected to evaluate the methodologies form two broad lines of inquiry: variables related to decision support and variables related to the phenomenon of insurgency. As outlined in the Literature Review, the decision support variables include the national interest, mandate, popular will, capability to act, and risk. The phenomenon of insurgency variables include relative deprivation, insurgency category, insurgent strategy, life cycle stage, external support, sanctuary, redress of grievances, and population control. The evaluation will rate the degree to which the methodologies illuminate each criterion. For example, a methodology that excels at illuminating the national interest will score "high." One that does so poorly will score "low." One that does not address the criterion will score "N/A - not applicable."

These assessments are subjective. The ratings represent the study findings based upon the application of the methodology to the case studies.

Decision Support Variables

Table 2: Decision Support Variable Evaluation Results

Criterion	Interagency Conflict Assessment Framework	Army Design Methodology	Guide for the Analysis of Insurgency
National Interest	Low	Low	N/A
Mandate	Low	Low	N/A
Popular Will	High	Low	Low
Capability to Act	High	Low	Low
Risk	High	High	Low

Source: Created by author.

National Interest

None of the methodologies demonstrated significant capability to illuminate the national interest. The GAI reflects deliberate ignorance of the national interest. This ignorance should not be viewed pejoratively; this trait allows the methodology to render balanced assessments agnostic of the US position within a conflict. The ICAF and ADM, on the other hand take the approach of assuming that planning to intervene in some fashion serves the national interest, fait accompli. The ICAF and ADM might allow for inclusion of that sort of information within a system map, but neither provides explicit or implicit intellectual resources to consider national interest.

Mandate

Similar to the previous criterion, no approach demonstrated significant capability. The GAI ignores mandate as outside of its scope. The ICAF and ADM leave the possibility of consideration open, but provide no impetus to examine a mandate for action.

Popular Will

The ICAF illuminates the issue of popular will in two ways. First, during system mapping and core grievance identification process, it considers population sentiment. Second, during the window of vulnerability and window of opportunity process, the practitioner must consider the receptivity of the populace. The GAI also rates high against this criterion. In numerous places, it assesses the nature of popular identities, their grievances, and opportunities for redress within the system and outside of it. It stops short of explicitly calling for a review of popular will for intervention, but it advances the conversation throughout. The ADM ranks low because it lacks any specific methodological preoccupation with popular will. In spite of that fact, practitioners who diagram the current state and desired state properly may find themselves effectively addressing the question of popular will.

Capability to Act

On the question of capability to act, the ICAF again scores high. This owes to the consideration of windows of vulnerability and windows of opportunity. Those considerations set the stage for a productive discussion on entry points to the conflict. The ADM and GAI also provide some added value. The ADM helps by outlining the possible operational approach of the insurgency. If the practitioner then reverses the analysis and conducts the ADM from the perspective of a potential US intervention force, the value goes up. For its part, the GAI depicts capability to act by providing a sound description of the insurgency's capabilities. With that understanding in place, the policymaker can make a meaningful assessment of the United States' ability to positively influence the situation.

Risk

On the subject of risk, the more conceptual methodologies - the ICAF and the ADM - outshine the GAI. The ICAF performs well by anticipating the planning requirements needed to feed task two of the process. Delineating vulnerabilities and opportunities again pays dividends. The ADM assesses risk well because it provides a continuation of the current state into the future. The practitioner can therefore hint at the trajectory of the conflict and demonstrate where the insurgency might threaten US objectives, at least as far as they reveal themselves. The GAI does hint at trajectory of the conflict, but it represents a snapshot of the insurgency in time. The principal value comes from the net assessment and its ability to predict winners from present data.

Phenomenon of Insurgency Variables

Table 3: Phenomenon of Insurgency Variable Evaluation Results

Criterion	Interagency Conflict Assessment Framework	Army Design Methodology	Guide for the Analysis of Insurgency
Relative Deprivation	High	High	High
Insurgency Category	Low	Low	High
Insurgent Strategy	Low	High	High
Life Cycle Stage	Low	Low	High
External Support	High	High	High
Sanctuary	Low	Low	High
Redress of Grievance	High	Low	High
Population Control	Low	Low	High

Source: Created by author

Relative Deprivation

Each methodology illuminates relative deprivation within a conflict in its own way. The ICAF begins to comprehend this factor by mapping the system. It further builds understanding by considering threats to identity groups and societal patterns that mitigate and reinforce the conflict. The ADM shows relative deprivation best through its system study. Depicting the interaction of various actors shows which parties suffer at the hands of which others. The GAI approaches relative deprivation by clarifying grievances and in the willingness of the state to address grievances.

Insurgency Category

Only the GAI specifically considers insurgent category. By examining the insurgent approach the other two may allow the seasoned practitioner to infer insurgent category, but they provide no specific devices for addressing this criterion.

Insurgent Strategy

Both the ADM and the GAI effectively shed light on insurgency strategy. The GAI does so explicitly. The ADM gets the same effect by following the insurgent narrative and rationale through to its likely operational approach. From this information the strategy becomes evident. The ICAF provides some insight in a subroutine of the understand core grievances step. It instructs the practitioner to determine the actors' objectives, means and resources. Done properly, this step will generate an approximation of insurgent strategy.

Life Cycle Stage

Here again, only the GAI addresses the life cycle stage of an insurgency. It does so explicitly. The ICAF and ADM can facilitate that understanding, but only when conducted by a practitioner motivated to seek that information by aggregating the insurgent actions and drawing the conclusion.

External Support

All three methodologies facilitate understanding of external support, but they do so in different ways. The GAI specifically addresses external support, but it goes further to address the constraints that this support places upon either the government or the insurgency. The ICAF and the ADM both recommend system mapping as a means to understanding the context of the conflict. In this study, system mapping routinely led to understanding of external support.

Sanctuary

On the question of sanctuary for insurgents, the GAI again explicitly addresses the matter where the ICAF and ADM only indirectly bring out that information. Again, it is the system mapping function that provides the user the opportunity to show instances of sanctuary.

Redress of Grievances

The ICAF and GAI both excel at illuminating redress of grievances. The ICAF does this in parts of steps two and three of task one: understanding core grievances, and identify patterns reinforcing and mitigating conflict. The GAI addresses redress explicitly in its review of government characteristics. The ADM does not address the matter explicitly, but the study of interactions within the environment may yield insights.

Population Control

The GAI addresses population control. Not only does it address numerous aspects of the insurgent force and government security forces, but it also specifically queries the method of population control. It therefore scores high on this criterion. Both the ICAF and the ADM lack specific treatment of the subject. In spite of this, both methodologies retain the capacity to address population control indirectly.

If a man has good corn or wood, or boards, or pigs, to sell, or can make better chairs or knives, crucibles or church organs, than anybody else, you will find a broad hard-beaten road to his house, though it be in the woods.

—Ralph Waldo Emerson

CONCLUSION

This monograph set out to determine how the military should perform assessments of insurgencies before the commitment to military operations. It tested the Interagency Conflict Assessment Framework, the Guide for the Analysis of Insurgency, and the Army Design Methodology. It applied these frameworks to three active insurgencies: Boko Haram of Nigeria, the Movement for the Emancipation of the Niger Delta of Nigeria, and the National Movement for the Liberation of Azawad of Mali. The analytical and synthetic elements contained in the study do not support the original hypothesis that the ICAF is the best methodology for the task. It does support partially, in that the ICAF forms the most useful basis, but the original hypothesis failed to forecast the importance of a detailed assessment component and an integrated approach.

Conclusions

This study argues that a conceptual understanding of an insurgency is the *sine qua non* of phase zero insurgency assessments. Therefore the conceptual frameworks provide the ideal starting point. Of the two, the ICAF provides slightly more utility on this task. It does so for two reasons. First, the bulk of the interagency community uses the ICAF, whereas only the U.S. Army uses the ADM routinely. The ICAF then gives a better basis for common understanding. Second, while the ADM solves a variety of problems well, the ICAF was specifically designed to assess conflicts in progress. The authors built in certain features that help guide the practitioner to the most useful types of answers.

Additionally, this study finds that whenever possible, an insurgency assessment should use both conceptual and detail oriented tools. The best practice is to use an approach blended from the ICAF and the GAI. This blend achieves what the US Army calls "integrated planning." In practice, concepts will drive details while details influence concepts.[98] The combination of conceptual and detailed planning achieves synergy; the combination of approaches reveals insights that neither approach would reveal on its own.

<u>Recommendations</u>

Practitioners of phase zero insurgency assessments should take an integrated approach to the process, incorporating both conceptual and detailed assessments. In particular, this study recommends that the assessment begin with the ICAF, but build in the GAI as a subroutine of task one, step two: understand core grievances and social/institutional resilience.

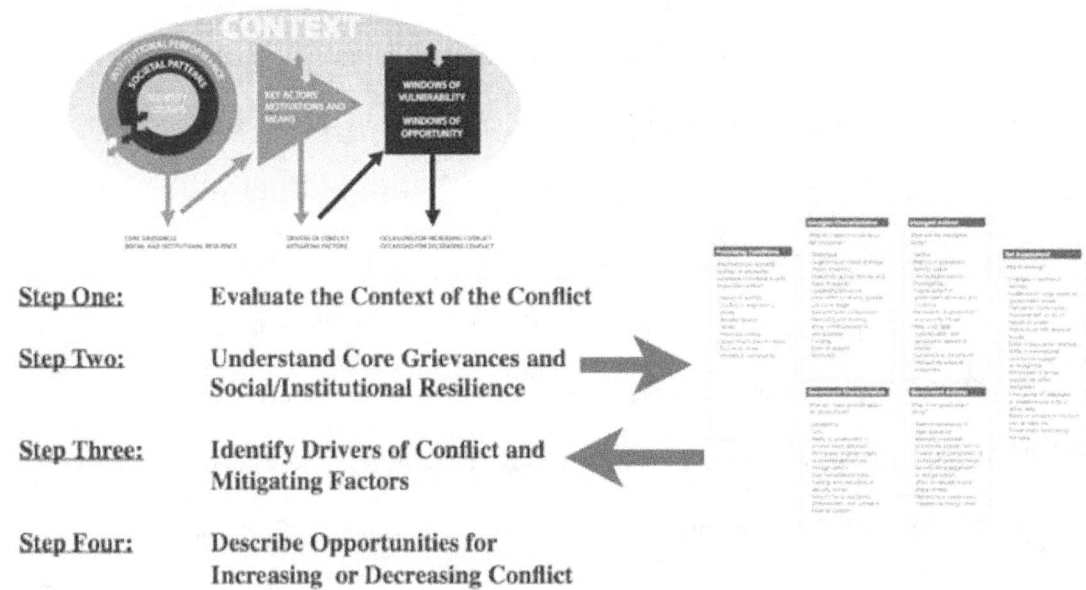

Figure 4: ICAF and GAI Blended Approach Process Diagram

Source: Author generated, from: United States Department of State, Office of the Coordinator for Reconstruction and Stabilization, *The Interagency Conflict Assessment Framework* (Washington, D.C.: S/CRS, 2008), 7; U.S. Central Intelligence Agency, *Guide to the Analysis of Insurgency* (Washington, DC: Central Intelligence Agency, 2012), preface, https://www.hsdl.org/?view&did=713599 (accessed November 21, 2013).

---

[98]U.S. Army, Army Doctrine Reference Publication 5-0, The Operations Process, 143.

The process benefits in two ways. The detail focus of the GAI sharpens the usefulness of the ICAF and provides insights that might remain hidden in its absence. Additionally, the focus on pragmatic concerns of planning gives the GAI a more utilitarian edge. The result is a simultaneous contemplation of the forest and its trees. The use of the ICAF to house all analysis ensures that the assessment will integrate seamlessly with the efforts of other agencies.

Topics For Further Study

Questions remain about the criteria selected for evaluation. This monograph utilized two sets of evaluation criteria: decision utility factors and phenomenon of insurgency factors. In order to scope the study in a manageable way, limited attention was given to analyzing the selection of these criteria. If scope were not a factor, each of these sets of criteria would warrant further study, or perhaps an entirely separate study. For example, to arrive at the policymaker utility criteria, select speeches were used to establish a baseline of critical inputs. A substantial body of decision making research exists that could challenge or augment the criteria chosen for this study. Additionally, the criteria chosen to evaluate the methodologies' grasp of the phenomenon of insurgency adapted piece-meal concepts from influential works in the field. Another study might begin with a mandate to generate those criteria from a broader survey of insurgency literature. Finally, the study gave limited attention to the study of complexity theory and the impact on insurgency assessments. That limited attention may have undersold an important aspect for evaluation.

BIBLIOGRAPHY

Binnendijk, Hans, and Patrick M. Cronin, eds. *Civilian Surge: Key to Complex Operations*. Washington, DC: National Defense University Press, 2009.

Boot, Max. *Invisible Armies Insurgency Tracker*. Council on Foreign Relations, 2013. http://www.cfr.org/wars-and-warfare/invisible-armies-insurgency-tracker/p29917 (accessed September 25, 2013).

Buchanan, Richard. "Best Defense: Is the Army Design Methodology Over Designed." foreignpolicy.com. November 1, 2012. http://ricks.foreignpolicy.com/posts/2012/11/01/ is_army_design_methodology_over_designed_there_are_trust_issues_too (accessed February 7, 2014).

Campbell, Dugald *On the Trail of the Veiled Tuareg*. London, UK: Seeley, Service and Company, 1928.

Carpenter, Ted Galen. *U.S. Aid to Anti-Communist Rebels: The "Reagan Doctrine" and Its Pitfalls*. Washington, DC: CATO Institute, 1986. http://www.cato.org/pubs/ pas/pa074es.html (accessed November 20, 2014).

Clarke, Michael. *An Insight Into Jihadist Strategy in the Sahel*. London, UK: Royal United Services Institute, 2013. https://www.rusi.org/analysis/commentary/ref: C511D272D72DDC/#.UyO9MKm_k20 (accessed January 14, 2014).

Connable, Ben, and Martin C. Libicki. *How Insurgencies End*. Santa Monica, CA: RAND Corporation, 2010.

Country Reports On Terrorism 2012. Washington, DC: United States Department of State, May 2013. http://www.state.gov/j/ct/rls/crt/2012/209979.htm (accessed November 20, 2013).

Dolan, Chris. *Social Torture: the Case of Northern Uganda, 1986-2006*. New York: Berghahn Books, 2009.

Eichstaedt, Peter. *First Kill Your Family: Child Soldiers of Uganda and the Lord's Resistance Army*. Chicago, IL: Chicago Review Press, 2009.

Forest, James. *Confronting the Terrorism of Boko Haram in Nigeria*. Tampa, FL: Joint Special Operations University, 2012.

Francis, David. *The Regional Impact of the Armed Conflict and French Intervention in Mali*. Oslo, NO: Norwegian Peacebuilding Resource Centre, 2013. http://www.peacebuilding.no/var/ezflow_site/storage/original/application/f18726c3338e3 9049bd4d554d4a22c36.pdf (accessed March 14, 2014).

Gharajedaghi, Jamshid. *Systems Thinking: Managing Chaos and Complexity*. 2nd ed. Amsterdam, NL: Elsevier, 2006.

Guevara, Che. *Guerrilla Warfare*. Lincoln: University of Nebraska Press, 1985.

Gurr, Ted Robert *Peoples Versus States: Minorities at Risk in the New Century*. Washington, DC: United States Institute of Peace, 2000.

———— *Why Men Rebel*. Princeton, NJ: Princeton University Press, 1970.

Hanson, Stephanie. *MEND*. Council on Foreign Relations, 2007. http://www.cfr.org/nigeria/mend-niger-deltas-umbrella-militant-group/p12920 (accessed November 10, 2013).

Irmer, Cynthia. "A Systems Approach and the Interagency Conflict Assessment Framework (ICAF)," paper presented at The Cornwallis Group XIV Workshop: Analysis of Societal Conflict and Counter-Insurgency. Vienna, Austria, 2009. http://www.thecornwallisgroup.org/workshop_2009.php (accessed 22 September 2013).

Junger, Sebastian. "Blood Oil." *Vanity Fair*, February 2007. http://www.vanityfair.com/politics/features/2007/02/junger200702 (accessed September 14, 2013).

Kalyvas, Stathis N. *The Logic of Violence in Civil War*. Cambridge Studies in Comparative Politics. Cambridge, UK: Cambridge University Press, 2006.

Kaplan, Jeffrey. *Terrorist Groups and the New Tribalism: Terrorism's Fifth Wave (political Violence)*. Reprint ed. New York: Routledge, 2012.

Keita, LTC Kalifa. "Conflict and Conflict Resolution in the Sahel: The Tuareg Insurgency in Mali." Master's thesis, U.S. Army War College, 1998. In Federal Depository Library Program Electronic Collection, http://permanent.access.gpo.gov/lps12312/carlisle-www.army.mil/usassi/ssipubs/pubs98/tuareg/tuareg.pdf (accessed October 22, 2013).

Kilcullen, David *The Accidental Guerrilla: Fighting Small Wars in the Midst of a Big One*. Oxford, UK: Oxford University Press, 2009.

Killing at Will: Extrajudicial Executions and Other Unlawful Killings by the Police In. London, UK: Amnesty International, 2009. http://www.amnesty.org/en/library/asset/ AFR44/038/2009/en/f09b1c15-77b4-40aa-a608-b3b01bde0fc5/afr440382009en.pdf (accessed January 6, 2014).

Lawson, Bryan. *How Designers Think: The Design Process Demystified*. 4th ed. Oxford, UK: Elsevier/Architectural, 2006.

LeSage, Andre. "Countering the Lord's Resistance Army in Central Africa." *Strategic Forum* 270 (July 2011). http://www.ndu.edu/press/lib/pdf/StrForum/SF-270.pdf (accessed November 2, 2013).

Mansoor, COL Peter, and MAJ Mark Ullrich. "Linking Doctrine to Action: A New Coin Center of Gravity Analysis." *Military Review* 87, no. 5 (September-October 2007): 45-51.

McLoughlin, Gerald, and Clarence J. Bouchat. *Nigerian Unity: in the Balance*. Carlisle, PA: SSI, 2013.

"NATO and the Scourge of Terrorism." NATO.int. February 18, 2005. Accessed February 5, 2014. http://www.nato.int/terrorism/five.htm.

Northern Nigeria: Background to Conflict. Washington, DC: International Crisis Group, 2010. http://www.crisisgroup.org/~/media/Files/africa/west-africa/nigeria/168%20Northern%20Nigeria%20-%20Background%20to%20Conflict.pdf (accessed January 15, 2014).

Obama, Barack. *National Security Strategy: May 2010.* Washington, DC: United States government, 2010. http://www.whitehouse.gov/sites/default/files/rss_viewer/national_security_strategy.pdf (accessed October 1, 2013).

————. "Remarks by the President in Address to the Nation on Libya." Speech, National Defense University, Washington, DC, March 28, 2011. http://www.whitehouse.gov/the-press-office/2011/03/28/remarks-president-address-nation-libya (accessed October 5, 2013).

————. "Remarks by the President in Address to the Nation On Syria." Speech, White House, Washington, DC, September 10, 2013. http://www.whitehouse.gov/the-press-office/2013/09/10/remarks-president-address-nation-syria (accessed October 5, 2013).

O'Neill, Bard E. *Insurgency and Terrorism: from Revolution to Apocalypse.* 2nd ed. Washington, DC: Potomac Books Inc., 2005.

Pham, J. Peter. *Africa Security Brief: Boko Haram's Evolving Threat.* Washington, DC: Africa Center for Strategic Studies, 2012. http://africacenter.org/wp-content/uploads/2012/04/AfricaBriefFinal_20.pdf (accessed March 8, 2014).

Poole, MAJ Anthony. "The Interagency Conflict Assessment Framework: A Pragmatic Tool for Army Design." Master's thesis, School of Advanced Military Studies, 2010. In Combined Arms Research Library Digital Library, http://cgsc.contentdm.oclc.org/cdm/ref/collection/p4013coll3/id/2687 (accessed September 3, 2013).

Rabasa, Angel, John Gordon IV, Peter Chalk, Christopher S. Chivvis, and Audra K. Grant. *From Insurgency to Stability.* Santa Monica, CA: RAND Corporation, 2011.

Sergie, Mohammed Aly, and Toni Johnson. *Boko Haram: Backgrounder.* New York: Council on Foreign Relations, 2014. http://www.cfr.org/nigeria/boko-haram/p25739 (accessed November 28, 2013).

Situation in Mali: Article 53(1) Report. The Hague, NL: International Criminal Court, 2013. http://www.icc-cpi.int/en_menus/icc/situations%20and%20cases/situations/icc0112/Documents/SASMaliArticle53_1PublicReportENG16Jan2013.pdf (accessed January 2, 2014).

Smith, Dane. *Foreign Assistance for Peace: The U.S. Agency for International Development.* Washington, DC: Center for Strategic and International Studies, 2009. Accessed January 10, 2014. http://www.voltairenet.org/IMG/pdf/USAID.pdf.

Smith, Daniel Jordan. *A Culture of Corruption: Everyday Deception and Popular Discontent in Nigeria*. Princeton: Princeton University Press, 2007.

Sustaining U.S. Global Leadership: Priorities for 21st Century Defense. Washington, DC: United States Department of Defense, 2012. http://www.defense.gov/news/defense_strategic_guidance.pdf (accessed November 21, 2013).

Taber, Robert. *The War of the Flea*. New York, NY: Lyle Stuart, 1965.

Terrorist Organization Profile: Lord's Resistance Army. College Park, MD: National Consortium for the Study of Terrorism and Responses to Terroism, 2013. http://www.start.umd.edu/start/data_collections/tops/terrorist_organization_profile.asp?id =3513 (accessed November 21, 2013).

The Economist. The Spreading Northern Insurgency. January 14, 2012.

The Swamps of Insurgency: Nigeria's Delta Unrest. International Crisis Group, 2006. http://www.crisisgroup.org/en/regions/africa/west-africa/nigeria/115-the-swamps-of-insurgency-nigerias-delta-unrest.aspx (accessed November 21, 2013).

Turabian, Kate L. *A Manual for Writers of Research Papers, Theses, and Dissertations: Chicago Style for Students and Researchers*. 7th ed. Chicago: University Of Chicago Press, 2007.

U.S. Army. Army Doctrine Publication 3-0, Operations. Washington, D.C.: Headquarters, Department of the Army, 2011.

———. Army Doctrine Publication 5-0, The Operations Process. Washington, D.C.: Headquarters, Department of the Army, 2012.

———. Army Doctrine Reference Publication 3-0, Operations. Washington, D.C.: Headquarters, Department of the Army, 2012.

———. Army Doctrine Reference Publication 5-0, The Operations Process. Washington, D.C.: Headquarters, Department of the Army, 2012.

———. *Art of Design: Student Text, Version 2.0*. Fort Leavenworth, KS: United States Army Command and General Staff College, 2010. http://usacac.army.mil/cac2/cgsc/events/sams/artofdesign_v2.pdf (accessed February 17, 2014).

———. Training and Doctrine Command Pamphlet 525-5-500, *Commander's Appreciation and Campaign Design*. Washington, D.C.: Headquarters, Department of the Army, 2008.

U.S. Central Intelligence Agency. *Guide the Analysis of Insurgency*. Washington, DC: Central Intelligence Agency, undated. https://www.hsdl.org/?view&did=230206 (accessed November 21, 2013).

———. *Guide to the Analysis of Insurgency*. Washington, DC: Central Intelligence Agency, 2012. https://www.hsdl.org/?view&did=713599. (accessed November 21, 2013).

U.S. Department of State, Office of the Coordinator for Reconstruction and Stabilization. The Interagency Conflict Assessment Framework. Washington, D.C.: S/CRS, 2008.

————. "Philippines: Looking at Mindanao." *ICAF Report.* January 2011. http://www.state.gov/documents/organization/187972.pdf (accessed 10 January 2014).

Vego, Milan. "A Case Against Systemic Operational Design." *Joint Forces Quarterly* 53, no. 2 (2nd Quarter 2009): 69-75.

Wilson, MAJ James. "Improving the Interagency Conflict Assessment Framework (ICAF) with Intellectual Habits." Master's thesis, Command and General Staff College, 2012. In Combined Arms Research Library Digital Library, http://cgsc.contentdm.oclc.org/cdm/ref/collection/p4013coll2/id/2917 (accessed October 17, 2013).

www.ingramcontent.com/pod-product-compliance
Lightning Source LLC
Chambersburg PA
CBHW080535290526
45790CB00006B/2417